# PARANOIA
# The Strange Case Of Ghosts, Demons And Aliens

By Christopher Saint Booth

SECOND EDITION
REVISED V2

ISBN-10: 0692488901
ISBN-13: 978-0692488904


Cover art design and layout: Christopher Saint Booth
Model: Rachel Marie

Editor: Denise Mendenhall



SPOOKED TV PUBLICATIONS
18017 CHATSWORTH STREET #130
GRANADA HILLS, CA 91344
Email: info@spookedproductions.com
Phone: 310-498-9576

# A VOID

*~In the beginning, I believed the sun and moon was God's eyes, air was our Lord's breath and rain was his tears of joy. I would shout out, "How beautiful we are"as 'God made man in his own image.'*

*~In the end, I couldn't see the sun or moon from all the global damage we had done, God's eyes had gone blind. The air was on fire which took our Lord's breath and left us flooded by his never ending tears of pain and war. I shouted out, "How ugly we are," as I realize 'Man has now made God in his own image.'*

Christopher Saint Booth

# THE STRANGE CASE INDEX

## FORWARD
By: Rachel Marie Booth


How can I sum up the life of Christopher Saint Booth? All I can say, there will never be enough words in the world to describe how truly amazing and talented he is.

This book is a testament of all his hard work and proves that if you want something bad enough, you can work your fooking butt off to get it.

In the time I have known Christopher, he has shown the world love, kindness and happiness. His motive in life is to show that love and light is the only path to follow in this world of darkness and destruction. How many people can you say, "Not only are you my friend but you are a shining light in the darkness?" Thank you for being a light, having strength and showing kindness to all those around you.


I hope everyone that reads this fantastic book sees the light and love that I see.


Christopher is a rare one-of-a-kind man and I am so proud of him!

# INTRODUCTION

It has always been a passion of mine to be a storyteller of the unique, the different and the underdog. Life's wrinkles and imperfections is my cup of tea. Whether a person is young or old, I could see it in their eyes that everyone dies but not everyone lives. These untold stories needed to be told. No doubt the paranormal realm is a personal thing, what someone believes, others may not.

So where do I even begin to tell you about my strange paranormal journey. How can I express the importance of how these haunting experiences of the afterlife has put meaning to my everyday life?

*Well how about from the beginning.....*

# THE STRANGE CASE OF TWINS

When I was around 10 years old Philip, my identical twin brother and I witnessed our first paranormal experience. I definitely would call it that, as there in no other radical explanation. Being twins, Philip and I shared almost everything when we were young. Clothes, toys, food and bedrooms. We even had joint custody to Pink Floyd's "The Wall" being that it was a double album. I believe Philip was gifted side one and two and I held the rights to sides three and the flip side. I don't think Philip and I ever got over the fact we shared a bloody album. Definitely a devastating experience for a competitive duo.

One night we had gone to bed early and I remember both of us waking up screaming. Our cute boy pajamas were sweaty as we were looking at each other in disbelief, trying to get some validation of what we had just seen. Upon the white closet doors that laid in front of our twin beds, as if it was a projector screen, played out our haunted nightmare.

A scene of the old English country side and a tent lit up the room. Out of this tent, a grey haired old lady appeared followed by a small white dog. She moved as if she was in slow motion, dragging along her grey attire covered in soot. Dressed in period clothing, her shawl was tattered and was wrapped tightly around her shoulders. Over yonder we could see a faded street sign with the name "Holmes Road."

As the dog ran ahead the white haired apparition turned and stared directly into our twin eyes and said *"It's ok, don't be afraid, I'm home now."* She had a warm smile reminiscent to one we had seen before. As she continued to move closer, she whispered, *"Tell your Mum, I'll see her soon."* Philip and I both screamed an identical shriek that echoed throughout our little house on Carey Road. Suddenly our bedroom door flew open and it was our Mum coming to the rescue. Out of breath she yelled *"What on Earth is going on? Dear Lord you almost scared me to death."* We began to tell her about what we had seen. Our Mum went quiet as she listened to our story. With tears in her eyes she began to tell her own story.

*"Boys, what you saw sounds like the countryside where you were born. The street sign, 'Holmes Road' was where your Grandparents lived. The small white dog was that of your Grandfather's and the grey haired old lady, I believe is your Grandmother and she died just a few hours ago."*

Boom! The room went silent, so quiet you could hear a pin drop. How could we remember this as we were only four years old the last time we saw our Grandparents? Also how did Philip and I have the same vision at the exact same time, just as our Grand-mum passed away? It was like our Grand-mum visited us to say goodbye. I have heard of this kind of thing before, of a loved one visiting just after their death. Yet I would of never believed it if it wasn't for the fact that we both had seen it with our own four eyes. It is said that twins can experience the same thoughts and feelings. Could it be possible that we also share the same 'spectral visitations' as well?

*In memory of our Grand-mum*

# THE STRANGE CASE OF LOS ANGELES

Fast Forward 15 years...

    The city of Angels, a land of traffic jams and broken dreams. Welcome to Hollywood! Philip and I dared move here to be rock stars. Musicians since the age of 13, we were destined to be noticed whether it was from our outlandish fashion style or the obsession I had for David Bowie, which grew to the point that my hair became spiky orange and my eyebrows disappeared by the blades of a razor. We just wanted to be different, you see we just couldn't fit in. Mum would say all the time *"Why can't you just be normal?"*

    Normal or paranormal, my passion led me to become the lead singer of "Sweeney Todd" in which I replaced Bryan Adams as the front man. London recording artists, gold records, Juno Award Winners and sold out shows. I had a lifestyle that would be hard to end. Along with my older brother Johnny B on drums, we set out on one of the longest tours across Canada.

    *"One should not fear the end when it's just something about to begin."* ~ *CSB*

    After the breakup of Sweeney Todd, Philip and I began

playing at the local clubs in Los Angeles. We played many of the legendary venues which included the Starwood, Rainbow, Roxy, Troubadour and the Whiskey. The Hollywood clubs were all about pay to play. I remembering them charging us for tap water in our dressing rooms. We could hardly afford hair spray never mind something to drink. Times were hard for musicians back then and even harder now, so making a living meant doing anything to survive. Even with the rock band, Mötley Crüe as our opening act (who was not famous at that time), it was hard to make ends meet. That said, I ended up laboring on Hollywood movies for $50.00 dollars a day in the art department. If they needed a ditch dug or a huge billboard moved, I was the one who did it. Long hours, low pay in California was called *'manuel labor'* meaning that not even the illegals would take on these jobs. But hey I was a still a musician supporting my art. Right? So, I did what I had to do.

I remember working with Charlton Heston and Jack Palance on the sci-fi film "Solar Crisis." In fact if you watch it, I'm the post-apocalyptic trumpet player at the bar. Originally commissioned to design all the futuristic instruments, due to my scruffy look they asked me to appear in the movie. I'm not sure if that was a compliment or not but it lead to my first acting role in a major motion picture.

During the filming of the drama driven movie, "Fear City" starring Tom Berenger and Melanie Griffith, I found the film's budget highlighting the overall costs and job descriptions on the soundstage floor at Raleigh Studios. Like a sign from above or at

12

least the Hollywood sign, I realized what we needed to do. It was time to get into film production and make our own movies. Phil and I had already became well versed in creating music videos and erotic thrillers for Playboy. They paid better than the indie films and though the scenery was better, the work was dirtier if you know what I mean. We made the stuff that people fast forwarded through when watching adult entertainment. Back then Playboy had bigger budgets, better production design and was more story driven than today. They were called Erotic Thrillers. We picked up over 11 Awards worldwide including Best Video, Best Editing, Best Cinematography, Best Music and Best Art Direction.

Whether I was working on feature films or adult films, there was not much difference as far as I was concerned. I gave it my all, putting passion in everything and treated every job professionally. For me, I was creating art, whether it was music, costuming or production design. During my time with Playboy, I met a lot of nice people, as well as many lost human beings whose spirit and dreams had been broken. I was happy to make these productions and the performers look good. It warmed my heart to see them transform, be more than they thought they could be. But eventually the productions got cheaper and the content got nastier. The truth is, it was too difficult on my ego and my psyche. I would arrive home after a long day of filming feeling very emotionally exhausted and depressed. I told myself we were making a real film but in reality it was not. I was a vegetarian at the time. I had quit drinking and didn't do drugs so I could see things crystal clear. I felt like the actors wore their troubles on the outside as I could see exactly who and what they were. My soul was becoming tarnished, it was time to move on.

# THE STRANGE CASE OF BEING JESUS

Many years back we shot a music video. It was called "Like Father, Like Son." The song was about my Dad. The music video was created from the idea of the ultimate father and son, God and his son Jesus. Whether you believe or not, it's a beautiful story of sacrifice and faith.

Our team set out to film in Joshua Tree, California where the scenery was similar to that of a biblical location. We filmed for 7 days and 7 nights. In our music video we covered Palm Sunday, the trial, the Stations of the Cross and the crucifixion. Out of all the shots we filmed, the crucifixion was the most powerful of them all. The weather remained good except for the last of day of filming which was the graphic crucifixion scene. I remember the clouds turning black, the rain poured down and lightening flashed. We could hear the rumble of thunder throughout our recordings.

It was time to act out the final scene to one of the most important stories of all time. The crew lifted me up onto the 12 foot wooden cross and strapped me in. Made by our prop and set department, it was an exact replica of what would have been used to crucify Jesus back in the day. I must admit I was extremely nervous. It was beyond frightening to act out this religious event. I meant no disrespect in the portrayal, yet I felt I needed to be careful about stepping on sacred ground.

As we started to film, the dark clouds opened up above

15

where I was mounted to the cross. Suddenly a beam of sunlight shone down illuminating me being crucified. My heart dropped with an overwhelming feeling of dread. I remember closing my eyes, even if it was just for a millisecond, I felt the humility, pain, sadness yet faith Jesus must have felt at that time of his sacrifice. It was an incredible life changing moment for me. As I came down from that splintered cross, things now seemed different. Everything was brighter, fresher and more vibrant. I felt a stronger connection to the Earth, its animals, people and the air that we breathe. People of faith would ask me,

*"How could I receive such a gift that others who have worshiped their whole life had not been given that one moment of true enlightenment?"*

I'm not sure what happened that day but that Nirvana changed my life. It made me love and care more about everything and everyone. The grass seemed more vibrant in shades of green I had never seen, the cows in the pasture gave off a human-like aura, I could see the air swirl and dance through the sky and smell the crisp, pure aroma as the wind blew past my face. If not for anything else that experience helped me cross my dear Mum as she would pass of cancer that same year.

I had seen the trees waving at me, vibrantly protecting themselves from earthly sickness. I had learned that the sap of a Yew Tree held a compound to a possible cure for cancer. I had

16

suggested that my Mum try this experimental drug, as time was running out. This serum of chance bought her a few extra months, which was more than anyone could ask from this horrific fight. Only then could she see the waving of the trees as I had, experiencing this new connection with God together as one.

My mother saw the light in me, the Nuns and hospice workers recognized my epiphany. Hand in hand, tear to tear we faced her transition to Heaven. She closed her eyes and the battle was over, finally she found peace. I will always remember when I portrayed Jesus, the day I turned 33 years old.

*In memory of Audrey Jackson Booth and Leslie Booth.*

# THE STRANGE CASE OF THE OLD SOLDIERS HOME

Thinking back on another indie film I worked on I seemed to have a knack of filming in creepy places. This time it was Twentieth Century Fox's "Dream Scape" starring Eddie Albert, Christopher Plummer and Dennis Quaid. The filming location was the old VA hospital in Westwood, known as "The Old Soldiers Home." It was my job description as well as a select few to do cleanup work for the on-screen dream hospital. For you IMDb fanatics my credited art director name is "Christof."

Working hard with the art department, it seemed that one of the psychotic patients had escaped from the newly built VA hospital next door and was hiding in the basement of this old VA hospital we were prepping. While scraping the paint from the floors I heard muffled screams through the ventilation shaft. It was a male voice repeating the words, "*I didn't mean to kill you Joe, I didn't mean to kill you.*" It sent shivers down my spine. Over and over again the mental cries grew. Scared and confused, I ran down the hospital corridors into something right out of a horror movie. Out of the darkness dead birds literally floated across the asylum's floor. At that point, all I could do is pick up the shovel that they supplied me with and start whacking these zombie fowls down. After my major freak out subsided, I realized these birds were not hovering across the floor at all. They were actually being carried by hundreds of creepy-crawly maggots to the corner of their choice. It was dinner time in the ole nut house and I was not hungry to say the least.

# THE STRANGE CASE OF DARKPLACE

Linda Vista Hospital is located in Boyle Heights on the outskirts of Los Angeles and is said to be one of LA's most haunted locations. Featured in many ghost reality shows it still perplexes my brain to understand why they call them reality shows, when there is nothing real about them at all. What was real is the fact that Philip and my first indie-horror film, "DarkPlace" was shot there starring the late Matthew McGrory (Tiny from "Devil's Rejects" and "House of 1000 Corpses.") This would be Matthew's last film as he would soon pass shortly after. I remember driving Matthew around on the set in my Range Rover. He was so tall (measuring at 7 feet, 6 inches) I had to remove the front passenger seat as he would need to sit in the back from needing excessive leg room. He was a beautiful man and is greatly missed. Bless him...

While at Linda Vista, the hospital was like a maze of institutional green hallways. The 5th floor was covered in six foot mounds of bird droppings which we nicknamed the land of the pigeons, (this would be the CDCs worst nightmare) making it sickening to explore.

While investigating we experienced cold spots, shadow people and even saw an apparition out of the corner of my eye. Many of the crew had seen a little girl lurking down the long burned out hallway. This was the time a fire took out one of the old hospital floors and elevators which in turn made a great location for our film. This place was an art director's dream. We gathered up all the left behind hospital equipment to make up our set including a shock therapy machine that our prop master ended up borrowing and using on himself for entertainment at parties.

Being that this hospital was truly haunted, Linda Vista made a great backdrop for our first supernatural horror film.

"DarkPlace" was released in 2007 and went on to win multiple awards at several prestigious film festivals worldwide including Nashville, Chicago and Germany for Best Horror Feature, Best Editing, Best Cinematography and Best Art Direction.

*In memory of Matthew McGrory*

# THE STRANGE CASE OF SPOOKED: THE GHOSTS OF WAVERLY HILLS SANATORIUM

The phone rang on what seemed to be another sunny day in the town that never rains. More than routine was on the Hollywood agenda. A producer we had previously worked with was on the phone pitching his new movie idea. The films synopsis was a story about cat burglars breaking into an art exhibit for a heist of the century. The location he wanted to use was an abandoned sanatorium in Kentucky. Apparently he and his brother used to break into it when they were kids. It was his mission to have Philip and I go down there, write the script and make the movie.

First rule of Independent filmmaking is to write your script around the location. So off I went, googling away to find out everything I could about this strange location so we could adapt it into the script. After searching on the Internet for days, I found a wealth of knowledge about this abandoned structure in Kentucky. It was called Waverly Hills Sanatorium and it had nothing to do with cat burglars, art exhibits or a heist of the century.

Research is everything when it comes to documenting the truth, especially when it comes to create entertaining projects that use marketing gimmicks such as *"based on true events."* Little did I know that what I was researching would not only be a huge turning point in my career but would also change my life. It was intriguing and yet scary as hell, for there is nothing scarier than the truth.

Waverly Hills Sanatorium was a place for hope and chances. But it was also a sad, desolate place filled with oppression and death for the many TB patients who did not find a cure. TB (short for tubercle bacillus) is known as Tuberculosis that is a disease caused by a bacterium called Mycobacterium Tuberculosis. The bacteria usually attacks the lungs, but TB bacteria can attack any part of the body such as the kidneys, spine, and brain. If not treated properly, TB disease can be fatal. Tuberculosis was once the leading cause of death in the United States. It was also known as the White Death and the White Plague.

What seems barbaric today was a common practice back then as many torturous operations were performed such as Thoracoplasty. The removal of ones ribs where only a few survived. Charles Mattingly owner of Waverly Hills explains in his Kentucky drawl:

*"What the operation consisted of was, they would cut open your rib cage and remove a few of your ribs. They would then take and collapse the lung that was in the worst shape keeping you calm as possible. They would have you breathe off of your good lung hoping that your other lung, while they had it collapsed would start to regenerate and get in better shape. Then they'd come back later and puff it back up and see if it the operation was successful."*

Charles Webster a Waverly Hills survivor remembers the

pain.

*"Right side, they took five ribs to collapse the lung. It makes you walk sideways because you're out of balance. You're always trying to favor that side. When I first had it done I was walking down the street sideways. Trying to get away from it I guess, the pain. That's a pretty good pain."*


This Sanatorium held a lot more then pain as Waverly Hills is known to be one of the most haunted places in the US. Plagued with ghost stories and folklore of dead patients still walking the halls today, the history seemed even more frightening,

Waverly Hills Sanatorium served as a Tuberculosis Hospital from October 17th of 1926 up until 1961. After that point it was closed down for approximately two years, remodeled and reopened as Woodhaven Geriatrics Center which was basically a nursing home, and it remained that until 1980 when it closed its doors for good. It also was known to have an enormous amount of deaths pass through its doors into the body chute. This was called the 'Death Tunnel.'


Ronald Parkhurst, a long time security guard for the abandoned hospital describes in detail.


*"The Body Chute, aka Death Tunnel is a 500 foot tunnel with a rail car system and cement steps that connects to the 1st floor of the main Kirkbride building and to the basement of the*

*original hospital. It was steam heated and it was used at one point
in time to bring supplies up. It was also used for employees to walk
up to get from the bottom of the hill in the winter months when it
was extremely cold and snow was deep. It had two rails just like a
railroad track in which carts were attached to move heavy objects.
At that time, there was a certain point during the Tuberculosis
epidemic that there were up to three people an hour dying. In
order to keep the patients from being demoralized at their own
kind of impending death the hospital staff would cart the bodies
out through the first floor to this tunnel, met with a conveyor belt
system that went 500 feet down towards the railroad tracks. There
the hearses and trains would pick up the bodies and take them
home to their family"*.

Mr. Thornberry a Waverly Hills worker states:

*"There never was but one hearse that ever came up to this
building. The doctor claimed that it upset a patient so bad that they
had a tunnel built and they put that dead wagon in there."*

# THE STRANGE CASE OF DEATH TUNNEL

Sporting my signature cowboy hat and a faux fur coat, off I flew from Los Angeles to Louisville, Kentucky. Arriving at Waverly Hills Sanatorium for the very first time, I must admit I was extremely blown away. It was like finding a sunken ship in the dessert. I was totally mesmerized yet scared shitless by this monster of a building. I had seen it only in pictures and now this gothic structure beckoned me to enter, if I dare.

There we met the local owners Charlie and Tina Mattingly. As they showed us around the abandoned property, we toured the five decaying floors with excitement. I felt like I was being watched, every hospital room had its own story. Eighty years of peeling paint, twisted walls, iron staircases and a morgue. You couldn't help but respect this deteriorating oasis for when you walked down the long institutional hallways one could only imagine what it was like back in the day. Now near extinction we were here to help save this crumbling location through exposure and donations.

Night fell on the old Sanatorium but the day wasn't over as we still had a lot of work to do. Out of the dark came an ominous figure, somewhat intimidating yet walked with a force to be seen. From the shadows to the moonlight, it was no other than rock & roll Ghost Hunter Keith Age.

Dressed in a leather vest, hat and jacket he seemed to be

26

protective of his turf. Age and his team the LGHS (Louisville Ghost Hunters Society) were the exclusive in-house investigators of Waverly Hills Sanatorium at that time. They had plenty of stories and evidence they soon would share. I told him and his team that we were here to film a horror movie and any help they could give us in explaining any paranormal disturbances, would be very much appreciated. The bearded hunter looked at his team, smiled and said, *"Welcome to my world."* After we told each other to *"Fuck off,"* Keith Age and I would soon become longtime friends and shoot seven more films together.

Keith went on to teach us more about the history of Waverly Hills Sanatorium and the reoccurring paranormal activity they had witnessed. He talked about shadow people, cold spots, EVPs and light abnormalities. His stories were bone chilling and the evidence they captured backed his claim. Intrigued and now awakened we started to document the possibility of the existence of ghosts, during our filming at Waverly.

We were there to scout and write a script but we also needed to figure out budget and logistics. For example, how were we going to run generator cables down through the 500 foot body chute to power our lights? The only source of light in this claustrophobic hole was from the small underground air vents above.

Philip the Director, Marcel the DP (Director of Photography) and I the Producer in the lead cautiously journeyed down this tunnel of death, every step being even scarier than the last. Of course it didn't help that all the hospital's history and ghost stories Keith told us about were now stuck in my head.

Finally reaching the bottom of the death tunnel, I looked behind me only to see that my crew-mates, Philip and Marcel had disappeared. They must have headed back up to home base. Suddenly a feeling of extreme darkness took over, a feeling of complete terror and desperation. Alone and now frightened, I felt like someone or something was standing right in front of me. I very much needed to get out of there and fast. I reached for my camera and snapped a picture and bolted up the dark tunnel with my video/audio recorder rolling. The run seemed endless as I was afraid to look back, scared that some monster may be chasing me.

Finally, I reached the top of the tunnel, out of breath, I collapsed and started to violently throw up. Something awful must have gone on down there, something very wicked indeed. I needed to figure out what the hell just happened. Hopefully I had caught something on my recorder.

Now back in Los Angeles. It was time to start production for this film. I loaded up the Waverly Hills scout pictures I had shot while on location and started the long process of reviewing them.

Suddenly that feeling of dread returned as I came across the picture I had taken at the bottom of the tunnel. The premonition of someone or something standing in front of me became quite clear. My photo revealed, a little girl with no eyes. Emerging from the dark shadows you could see her ghostly face, her long dark hair

28

and her black, hollowed out eyes. Truly frightening, she was like something out of a nightmare. Yet, I felt sorry for her as she projected feelings of sadness and loss. With a heavy heart I now dared to play the audio that was recorded that very day we were in the death tunnel.

The sound of screaming, cries from a young female being violently attacked filled the room. I could not help but put my hands over my ears and try and make it stop. The pain of not being able to help ripped me apart. Not only did I capture this ghost girl's picture and voice but possibly her death as well.

I was once told by a seasoned paranormal investigator, how do you know when you really got yourself a ghost?
* When you are able to get a picture.
* When you are able to get a voice, such as in an EVP.
* When you are able to feel a presence all around you.
When you get all three together, only then do you have yourself a "ghost."

You see it was the feeling of her presence, I experienced first that led me to take that picture and record sound.
Needless to say this art heist film we initially set out to write a script for, changed drastically.

I remember saying,

*"Whoa...all this stuff really happened, I mean really, really happened. Here is the script idea. All the history and the ghost stories, the people breaking in and all the twistedness that*

*went down. Let's make this movie about the real place."*

"Death Tunnel" and "Spooked - The Ghosts of Waverly Hills Sanatorium" was born.

I had spent over three years researching, documenting the history and haunting of Waverly Hills Sanatorium. Many nights alone, surrounded only by cameras trying to capture spirits to prove their existence.

Now don't expect to get paranormal evidence every time you investigate because it's not going to happen. But what is going to happen is you will get a better understanding of the ghost's story and the location's past. Then you can lock onto what is really happening, and have an honest direction on where to point your camera for your interviews.

A touching interview with a previous staff member, Mr. Thornbury solidified the local legend of Room 502 and the Nurse's aborted baby.

*"She made a mistake, got pregnant.... killed herself, they showed us where they found that baby."*

An elderly couple who had contracted Tuberculosis told us they felt like second class citizens and were treated like lepers. Some of the people we interviewed, this would be their last interview as they have passed on since. My memories of these dear souls is nothing short of being honored to tell their story. We smiled, laughed and cried together.

You can investigate all night and get nothing or immediately upon your arrival it can be a paranormal playground. Ghosts don't act on cue! It can be truly one of the most amazing experiences you will ever have or the most boring. In today's ghost reality TV shows, they are approximate 48 minutes or less for a one hour program. Within that hour they are made up of over 12 minutes of commercials or more. The show runners, editors and network are constantly trying to keep you from not changing the channel. So please take some of these shows with a grain of salt. It's entertainment not at its finest. We could expect a producer to yell on the set.

*"If you don't have a ghost in 20 minutes, find me one."*

Paranormal TV is not made for people in the paranormal industry, it is made for the average television viewer. I believe we need to have more faith and respect for the watchers of these shows. Trust that they will love the true compassionate side of ghost hunting as well as the scares. It goes back to 'balance.' Life is about balance and so is the afterlife. When something goes wrong it's usually the effect of something out of balance.

I remember after a long night of absent paranormal activity, leaning on a hospital's room wall and suddenly an old pair of shoes and hairbrush fell to the floor. Apparently hidden there in the patient's wall for safekeeping, it blew my mind. Holding the past artifacts and memories in my hands helped me to connect, not necessarily to who we were looking for but who might be looking for us. This would be communicated as energy to help the spirits close their story from unfinished business or lost goodbyes.

As a paranormal investigator, your soul mission is to help in any way you can but also respect what you cannot. Be compassionate and understand, you are in their house with their rules. We need hot like we need cold. We need life like we need the afterlife. Death is not final. The thought of dying and becoming a ghost, continuing on in limbo is an enlightening 'wakeup call' to say the least. You won't be able to mask life by taking a drink or lighting that bong when you're dead even though some might try. Heaven does not have parking spaces or storage units for your material possessions. We become what we have. What we are in life we are in death.

This is what paranormal storytelling is all about. Not your own reality show or the team with most evidence wins. It's about the history, the people and most of all it's about the spirits that linger on. We must fight to tell the real story, not full of lies.

*"After all, there is nothing scarier than the truth."*

I flew all the way from Kentucky to Los Angeles wearing the same cowboy boots I wore in the bloody body chute. I couldn't wait to get to the American Film Market and tell this chilling story to our dear friend Ray Cannella of Syfy.

When his mouth dropped open, I knew we had an outstanding, emotional adventure in the works. Ray always believed in us and the network loved the way we told our stories. It didn't matter how much evidence we captured, it was the human interest that captured their hearts. Within the Spooked documentary, we were able to validate the history, address the local legends, put a face to Mary the little girl on the third floor and give remembrance to the brave souls of Waverly Hills Sanatorium. All they wanted was to find a cure and it was our hope through our documentary they were able to find some kind of closure. The trials and tribulations of these poor souls will always be the stars of our films. They are a dedicated cast you will never forget.

Sony Pictures picked up "Death Tunnel" the movie and Syfy channel aired "Spooked The Ghosts Of Waverly Hills Sanatorium" the documentary for themselves. "Death Tunnel" was released worldwide and went on to be a cult film. "Spooked" received high TV ratings and became the poster child of all para-documentaries to come.

# THE STRANGE CASE OF CHILDREN OF THE GRAVE

When you have your own child as I was blessed to have, you will do anything to keep them safe and warm. You will sit up all night, rock them to sleep, even drive them around Walmart's parking lot. But when you are dealing with ghost children, how do we comfort them? It broke my heart trying, as a picture is worth a thousand words or souls when it comes to this chapter.

If there is ever a more lonesome word than orphanage, I could never imagine what that word might be.

*"If your parents aren't dead, they are now,"* they were told. *"You have no names, you are a number and an inmate of the Orphan Asylum."*

Some of the orphan homes where called asylums as well as the orphans were labeled inmates. A lot of them didn't have any names, they were just classified as numbers.

Stated in a letter attached to an orphan child, the cold reality hits hard.

*"By the love of God, please be so kind as to take this poor orphan in. And if she should die, please bury her for me, and I will be very happy. You can keep the baby or you can put it in the*

*street. By taking the poor child in the asylum, it has happily been saved from being murdered this morning by it's unfortunate mother."*

While appearing at the annual Mid-South Paranormal Conference. We had gotten a tip from Mary Ellen Hammack, an independent paranormal investigator. She told us of a heart breaking story of how 699 orphan children were buried in a mass grave at the Crown Hill Cemetery in Indianapolis. Slightly half of those 699 children that was buried were boys. Two thirds of the children were white, with their ages ranging from only a few months to fifteen years old. Research revealed they died from diphtheria, typhoid and other illnesses. Many apparently had also died from formaldehyde poisoning that was put in their milk they were served. When they thought they were nourishing these children, they were actually being poisoned.

As featured in this interview below from our "Children Of The Grave" documentary. Our paranormal team consisted of Mary Ellen Hammack, John Zaffis, Keith Age and Philip Adrian Booth.

Keith Age reports,

*"One thing that stuck out to me, in 1916, they said they had, I can't remember the exact number, 800 and something children were put into this Orphan Asylum and within six years 350 of them had died. 345 had died while in the custody, that's nearly 40 percent."*

Mary Ellen Hammack reports,

*"I have been informed that research has proven that many of these children were used in work houses. And in such poor conditions that many of them were served milk with formaldehyde. Which we believe is part of the reason why so many children here are buried secretly in unmarked graves."*

John Zaffis a paranormal researcher based in Connecticut, United States where he operates the Paranormal and Demonology Research Society of New England expressed his view.

*"Spirits of children. Why do they linger? Because they're confused, they're bewildered. They stay earthbound because they are looking for their parents. They're looking for their loved ones! And they will roam forever searching for these family members."*

Buried deep in the dirt of section 37 of the Indianapolis Crown Hill Cemetery, lies young Harry. An abused and neglected orphan. Harry's short life and tragic death in 1913 were all too familiar to the nearly 700 other abandoned orphan children buried there. But it wasn't until a young determined college intern started digging deeper into closed cemetery records, this is when the atrocity of section 37 came to light. 699 unmarked graves of 699 unwanted children.

Section 37, up on the hill in the cemetery is where these children now rest. It was very much alive with paranormal activity.

When we arrived we set up our cameras and we immediately captured an EVP (Electronic Voice Phenomenon) that we would never forget. Below is an audio transcription from our videotaping.

Philip Booth:
*"Oh my God. There was screaming!"*

Mary Ellen Hammack:
*"Is somebody talking to us?"*

Philip Booth:
*"I don't know but I'm picking something up. Screaming, people screaming."*

Keith Age:
*"Well at first we thought it was just interference, but I've never heard any type of interference like that before and I have done all kinds of sound engineering. This just sounded like a thousand people screaming at once."*

Rosemary Ellen Guiley, an American researcher and writer of books related to spirituality, the occult and the paranormal explains:

*"It is easier for children to become stuck than adults simply because they don't know what happened to them. They don't know where they are supposed to go. If they've been alone, if they've been mistreated, they may not understand even that they've died. So they're gonna want to hang around and stay in the same location that they're familiar with. They are usually ghosts associated with orphanages, asylums, homes for abandoned children. Quite often they were mistreated during the course of their lifetime. I think that the form and power of a haunting entity depends on a number of factors. One there is energy of place. What sort of energy that gets left behind. Other energies associated with ghost children are going to be less strong. They may be only to manifest as little glimmers of light for example. They may be able to only manifest an EVP or cause Interruptions of lights and malfunctions of equipment."*

The EVP we caught that day at Crow Hill Cemetery sounded like a thousand people screaming. It was an amazing capture as immediately after, all our equipment batteries went dead. It was a beginning to no end in the research of why these children remain trapped.

John Zaffis adds:

*"Children in mass burial graves. Is there confusion? Is that why they stay earthbound? Their graves aren't even marked. Could*

*this be why some of these children's spirits actually stay and haunt in these particular areas?"*

As we paid our respects it was time to move to our next location, Barton State Asylum in Peoria, Illinois. We had gone there to investigate the Bartonville cemetery where there were over a thousand forgotten souls buried in unnamed graves. Imagine all these graves with only numbers. A most desolate landscape of atrocity.

It was a rough few days at the old Peoria graveyard. As the clouds grew dark, the findings grew even darker. I felt a heavy feeling of unrest at this so called place of rest. Tugging on my heartstrings there was a sense of responsibility to find out who was buried here. Some of the gravestones had fallen over due to extreme weather conditions supported only by discards people had dumped into a ravine. Keith Age, Philip and myself did our best to replant some of the grave stones. I remember seeing several aging coffins unearthed covered in mud and trash. Treated very much like undesirables, many of today's cemeteries are left unkept with no financial assistance at all. Even under a court order the state of Illinois is not obligated to divulge who lie in those plots. The dead were property of Barton State Asylum and they were lucky that they were even buried never mind having a number instead of a name. Feeling frustrated at these ghastly findings, I couldn't seem to shake this investigation off. To clear our heads we decided to clean up at a local motel. Anxiety was hitting hard as we had to do another location scout that night. I felt like something was attached to me, could it possibly be a paranormal hitchhiker from the graveyard?

There wrapped around my cowboy boot was an old newspaper from the year, 1932. Was this a sign, was this some kind of message from beyond saying *"Don't forget me?"* I knew then and there that we must help, give tribute to these forgotten spirits by telling their story. As long as they were found I could deal with them being lost.

For a few years past, I have researched the most degraded people on earth. Composed of the children of poverty, vice, crime and degradation. These neglected, suffering crushed souls appeal to us as no others can. Their cry, the wail of perishing infancy and neglected childhood, has been heard. For what has been done to them we ask for mercy. God forgive us.

# THE STRANGE CASE OF ZOMBIE ROAD

Like most of us we get many emails per day. Well one stood out specifically. It included a photo of an unearthly sighting to say the least. My first reaction was this cannot be real, it had to be Photoshopped. So I examined it closely and could not find any trace of it being altered. This photo was taken by the late Tom Halstead. May he rest in peace.

Tom was a talented chap and funny too. He had a gift of spirit photography. This is when I met Paranormal Task Force, a dedicated team with pride and passion. Who would have thought that one photo would lead to an investigation of an (after) lifetime?

The submitted photo sent was of a hillside in the moonlight. On that hillside there were several barren trees. In between those trees there were silhouettes / shadows of what seemed to be ten or so small children standing there. Some had misshapen heads yet all were about four feet tall. At the bottom of the picture was a shallow pond where the moonlight and trees cast a mild reflection, but not the children. That was the strange part. There was absolutely no reflection of these mysterious shadow children. I have to say it was one of the best paranormal photos I had ever seen yet I was not totally convinced it was real. The Task Force explained to me that when this photo was taken there was no children on the hillside. There was no children in the area at all as it was a late night investigation in the woods. I then asked where

41

this picture was shot and the reply I got sent shivers down my British spine. "Zombie Road" they called it. With a name like that how could I resist? Can you say road trip? We did just that.

Six miles of broken road we traveled down into this forest of terror the locals called "Zombie Road." Located outside of St. Louis, Missouri it is actually a state park by the Meramec River which is Indian for "River of Death." A majority of the deaths that occur there now are from children drowning. There had also been reports of diphtheria, satanic rituals, suicides and murder. Known as a local "hot spot" for paranormal activity. Paranormal teams such as The Paranormal Task Force have captured shadow figures, light abnormalities, EVPs and even ghostly apparitions. This is a place so dangerous not even the St. Louis police department would accompany us on our investigation.

Escorted by an ex-military para-team with bulletproof vests, sensitives and camera crew we headed deep down into the woods. I definitely picked the wrong day to wear my new vintage army boots as my feet would surely remind me later. Half way down the Zombie path I could not help but notice the empty feeling these woods secreted. There were no sounds of night insects, animals or even a breeze. Only the sound of fear rang true. The deeper we got the scarier it became. Using the Thermal Imager, we were able to catch some shadow figures but it was not the shadow-nest we had been searching for as captured in Tom's photo. After all, that is what we came here for and we were not leaving until we found terrifying truth.

One of the things I found interesting about this specific investigation was the sounds we got on our audio recorders. Electronic Voice Phenomenon known as EVPs are sounds found on electronic recording equipment that are interpreted as spirit voices. EVPs have been around since the 1920's when Thomas Edison tried to invent a machine to talk with the dead. Today ghost hunters place tape and digital audio recorders in empty rooms in hopes to capture the voices of the deceased. EVPs usually occur between human conversations and can be interpreted as answers to questions asked by the paranormal investigator. But, these EVPs were different. They were more like alien rhythmic tones then voices of the dead. These mysterious tones would occur before we spoke. Almost like a reference pattern setting up our thoughts of what to say and then how to react. By these EVPs broadcasting a suggestive rhythmic pattern first, inaudible to the ear it may be a form of mind control or communication such as a telepathic cue card. Were these entities prompting us to find them or mislead us entirely to keep themselves hidden?

A rhythmic pattern sprang from our recordings revealing it was not "speech" at all but a murmured group of sounds (imagine instead of saying the words, humming them out loud) that suggested the sentence *"Look over there,"* moments later you could then hear me say, *"Look over there"* and our team did just that. We all looked over there. Behold, there on our Thermal Imager was the dark nest of shadows we had been looking for. Ten looming shadow children stood there watching us. We could not believe our eyes! Visible only by the

FLIR Thermal Imager as we could not see them with the human eye. This is one of the best captures of paranormal activity today.

FLIR (Forward Looking Infrared) cameras are a thermographic camera that senses infrared radiation and heat signatures. They create pictures from heat, not visible light. For paranormal application the concept is with color FLIR images, red usually means warm or hot (alive) while black depicts cold (dead).

The form and haunting of an entity depends on a number of factors. Sometimes a lot of energy gets left behind that is then going to be able to manifest in a much more dramatic way, perhaps a full bodied apparition or a very dramatic shadow figure.

In theory a shadow person, dark entity, black mass is known as a paranormal occurrence. That night we witnessed a black mass as well, something that every investigator is not comfortable about experiencing. Usually a small shadow person in general is written off as a ghost child. The majority of EVPs captured are those of children. These shadow Imps are often seen in haunted hospitals, asylums and houses. A majority of them in our findings have misshapen heads. Large in size compared to their body structure they are instantly labeled in many ghost hunter reality shows as dead children. With these pre-rhythmic alien EVP communications and these disfigured small shadow entities we captured, they may not be ghosts at all. Could they be extraterrestrials, something from an alien world hiding in the shadows studying us, waiting for the right time to make themselves known?

Makes you think, doesn't it?

Keith Age explains;

*'We've actually had these things walk through laser beams, set off motion detectors. You can take a laser beam, point it at them and as they move forward their mass blocks out the beam proving that they have some kind of substance. You can see the laser beam getting closer and closer and as the darkness gets closer, the temperature is dropping sometimes 20 to 30 degrees lower."*

Whether they are black masses, shadow people or extraterrestrials they all seem to have a solid structure. Laser beams do not cut through them.

After walking six miles back to home base, we were in total awe of what just had happened. I fell back on to the hotel room bed exhausted and just as I figured, my feet hurt like hell. It would be hard to sleep tonight knowing that these shadow things are indeed out there and very much alive.

"Children Of The Grave" was originally called. "Children Of The Damned" but was changed by the network. "Children Of The Grave" aired on the Syfy Channel and on Chiller TV to high ratings. Winner of best Paranormal Documentary. In memory of Tom Halstead.

# THE STRANGE CASE OF GORE ORPHANAGE

During our research of "Children Of The Grave" I came across a ghost story about the haunted Gore Orphanage. Finding no solid proof that there was ever an orphanage named Gore, I did however find a street named Gore Orphanage Road located in Vermillion, Ohio. The ghost story included, dead orphans turning into ash, gravestones made of burning embers and the screaming sound of children running for their lives. Legend has it that these children perished in a deliberate orphanage fire started by the caretaker Old Man Gore. Now these deceased orphans haunt the local woods.

Seeking more answers to this tragic tale, I set out to find the truth. Of course this story, like many was based on several true events that happened in the area. Such is the Collinwood School fire of 1908 that horribly took the lives of 172 children. The Swift Mansion children deaths said to be caused by diphtheria that dealt with spiritual séances trying to bring the sickly ones back from the dead. And last but not least the Light of Hope Orphanage fire. All these true events combined made up the infamous Gore Orphanage legend as we know it today. It is important to note that after the Collinwood School fire, public buildings went on to practice better fire safety due to the fact that the burnt school's exit doors opened inward meaning the fire brigade on the outside could not get in with all the bodies piled up inside behind the door. Truly tragic.

While researching the internet for more on this haunting ghost story, I came across a strange eBay ad. *"Haunted Arm For Sale Found In Gore Orphanage."* You can only imagine how I freaked out as I simultaneously clicked this link.

Apparently some chap who was cleaning out barns found an old trunk. In this trunk was a late 18 century prosthetic arm made of leather and rusted metal brackets. Equipped with a hook it appeared to be made for a child. A child that had lost his or her hand or forearm possibly to polio. A sad realization this must have been as I was already in tears channeling the agony through this child's eyes.

The eBay seller said the prosthetic arm was haunted and it needed to be kept locked away for good. Apparently when he had placed it in a vault for safe keeping, he would hear deep scratching sounds like it was trying to dig its way out. This story haunted me immensely but also tugged on my emotional side. So I immediately placed a bid in hopes to purchase this so I could protect the arm from any further exploitation. My heart raced with the idea of finding the family it belonged too as I did not believe the arm was haunted at all but I did believe that I needed to help save the spirit that may be attached to it and bring it closure.

$300.00 later, I won the bid. The description on the receipt was, *"Vintage artificial limb tormented haunted 100 years old."*

The seller shipped it to me immediately and to my surprise he included an antique book. The old book was from the turn of the century dated 1878 called "Mother, Home and Heaven." He told me that he found both the book and prosthetic arm together in the old trunk. The book was written by a Reverend and included poems for dying children. Reading these sad poems literally broke my heart. Every chapter lay a reminisce of a child's past. Inside this decaying book, there were page markers made of ribbon, pressed flowers and material of what seemed to be that of a little girl's dress. Even handwritten lead pencil markings of a little girls crush on her school teacher filled the once voided margins. Slowly turning the old deteriorating pages, I found the saddest memory of all, a golden lock of hair tied tightly with thread. A delicate yellow curl, softer than air, saved from a little ones first haircut or last. It was hard to continue at this point as this old book now seemed to resemble a personal diary of someone documenting their child's life and death. On the very last page inserted deep within the books spine was a strand of newborn baby's hair completing the final chapter as the books last words were, *"The End."*

I never did find the antique book or the arms original owner. The eBay seller has disappeared. To this day I keep these sad keepsakes together in a trunk, both safe until that one day I find their true heirs and as of yet the arm has not dug itself out.

*In memory of Brian K. Wilson Sr.*

# THE STRANGE CASE OF THE CRESCENT HOTEL

Winding stone staircases lead up to a gothic structure on top of a swollen hill. The view overlooked a "Twilight Zone" city full or crystals and artisans. Across the street lived the estranged caretaker aka tour guide when paranormal conventions came to town. Welcome to the Crescent Hotel in Eureka Springs, Arkansas know as one of the most haunted hotels in America. Built in 1886. This is where Philip and I would film our interviews for our para-doc "Children Of The Grave." The versatile cast included Steven La Chance, Greg Myers, Troy Taylor, Keith age and John Zaffis who at the time was also known as our "League of Paranormal Gentlemen." When author Rosemary Ellen Guiley joined the league, the empowering LOPG was not the correct descriptive so we disbanded the name.

The hotel was beautiful and yet spooky. The architecture was 19th century design full of aging antiques and relics from the past. The hallways was half-full with ghost tours echoing all kinds of grizzly stories including the crazed Dr. Norman Baker who apparently did horrific experiments on his cancerous patients. Claiming to cure them yet arrested for fraud, Dr. Baker would cut into his patient's skulls and inject his magical cure of spring water into their infected brains. It is said that over 420 patients died here.

While I'm pretty sure not all of these stories are

true, the place sure creeped me out.

When you are staying in the room that used to be the wicked Doctor's operating theater all kind of things go through your head. It must have been something about this mad man inserting animal parts into live patients that didn't make our night's sleep any easier. We pretty much slept with the lights on and our eyes half open, waiting for the Doctor to attack again.

Definitely put this on your paranormal bucket list or if you are spooked easily then put this on your fuckit list.

# THE STRANGE CASE OF THE WATSEKA WONDER

Based on a startling and instructive psychological study. The Watseka Wonder case was also classified as an authentic instance of Angelic visitation. All Spiritualists, and those investigating the subject of reincarnation will find this case a must read.

The small town of Watseka, Illinois population 5,000 is located about 50 miles south of Chicago and only a few miles from the Indiana border. The sensation that would come to be known as the Watseka Wonder had its beginnings there in July of 1877.

*"The Watseka Wonder story, America's first documented possession involving two stories and two families. The first family is the Roff family, they had a daughter, Mary Roff, who died mysteriously when she was 18 years old. Twelve years later in 1877, Lurancy Vennum, a girl who was 14 years old, and lived on the other side of town, who was only two years old when Mary Roff died. She began having her own series of fits and seizures along the same lines that Mary Roff had. At one point Lurancy told the people she was communicating with a spirit that wanted to come into her body, and it was someone who knew someone here in the town. When the spirit came into her body, and within a few days, Lurancy Vennum, or Lurancy under the power of Mary Roff, had*

*convinced the Roff family that she was indeed their dead daughter.*" ~John Whitman, Owner of the Watseka Wonder/ Roff House

It was almost winter and the moon was full. Talk about a panic attack driving up to Watseka in the dead of night. On each side of the old highway we were surrounded by miles of dying corn fields. Images of "Children of the Corn" stuck in my head as I had visions of being sickled to death. If we were going to run out of gas in the middle of nowhere and be killed, this is exactly where it would go down.

Upon arrival, Watseka was a cute little town that had a wonderful old museum and a classic movie theater. It also had a roach motel where we could rest and hide from the wicked corn monster. We slept for a few hours in the bug infested room. After a quick shower we headed to the first brick house in the Illinois County.

John Whitman owner of the Roff House agreed to open his doors with the promise that we would only tell the Watseka Wonder story accurately. With help from John and the talented researcher Juli Velazquez, we were able to interview the townspeople including the owner of the Lurancy Vennum house.

Arriving late at night, upon our knock, John greeted us politely and welcomed us into his historic home. I'm not sure if he was as excited to see us as we were him, but it was nice to finally put a face or in this case a house to the story we had been researching for months. I remember feeling dizzy, a little off balanced when we first entered. It was a sickening feeling of deep remorse. The house was void from furniture and the walls were bare. An old hollow staircase beckoned us to climb, yet the parlor was the initial centerpiece calling for our investigation.

In general parlors are used for receptions and formal events such as weddings, births and funerals. Yes, you guessed it. This is the room where they would show the body of the deceased. This is how the funeral parlor got its name. It was far too morbid to call it a Death Room. The name parlor was eventually discarded when families stopped having funerals in their homes. It was then changed to living room.

The ever-popular séances of that century were also held in the parlor and the Roffs' practiced this on many occasions. This meaning we would not be alone as there would be many spirits to entertain. Our Spirit box and other form of white noise communications in this room would prove later to be scary as hell.

Juli Velazquez, one of our team's paranormal investigators had caught some interesting evidence on "The Frank's Box." Invented in 2002 by Frank Sumption "The Frank's Box" is an instrumental trans-communication (ITC) device that allowed users to talk with the dead. The box sweeps radio bands and spirit voices supposedly echo through. Juli Velazquez explains;

*"The first time we did the audio at the Roff house we got*

*some very disturbing entities that seemed to be coming through the box. A lot of them were "Help me." When we asked certain things as if it was a crime an entity came over and said "Stop, that's enough." I didn't want to pursue the conversation as I felt they wanted to deter us, almost as if they had something to hide or a secret within the walls of this residence. We got approximately nineteen different types of segments that came through. Also, you have to understand that with the box you're not always hearing everything in real time. So we record everything that we do so we can go back and run through and section off each segment as you may have more than one entity that is coming through at a time. Someone who wants to tell a story, you might also get another entity that doesn't want them to tell a story. So you can actually hear intermingling, or conversations that are transpiring back and forth on the other side."*

I remember reviewing the Watseka Wonder case Electronic Voice Phenomenon back in our Los Angeles studio. There were no children at the Roff house when we recorded these EVPs as we do not allow kids on our investigations. But somehow we managed to capture the chilling voice of a young girl saying, *"Mommy why is Daddy doing this to me?"*

My heart broke as I analyzed the playback. What is one's human responsibility at that point? Do you brush it under the rug of do you try and do something about it and help? It haunted me deeply, the whole investigation did. There's more than meets the eye or in this case the ear going on here. That haunting EVP was enough for me to immediately schedule another visit to the Roff house and get to the bottom of what the Wonder was in Watseka.

Through "The Watseka Wonder" investigations we got over one hundred and eight EVPs. Sad unidentifiable voices of children whether caught at the Manteno asylum or at the house. Accompanied by Troy Taylor, Keith Age, my twin brother Philip and Bill Chappell, we set out on our final investigation. Bill of Digital Dowsing had designed some custom bio-feedback devices that would be later strapped on to Psychic Medium Rick Hayes. This savvy bunch of individuals made me feel proud, as they all came together for one reason, to help get closure to one of the most extraordinary cases of possession, or was it reincarnation?

*"It's one of the most unusual cases on record of spirit possession. Now three quarters of the world population believes in reincarnation. But the prevailing view is that you die and you come back into another life as an infant. Now here we have a case where a dead person stepped into the body of a young girl,"* explained Rosemary Ellen Guiley

We had taken Rick Hayes to the Roff house to see what he picked up.

*"Immediately when I arrived there I walked up on the porch and shared with the producers, The Booth Brothers, there*

*was a young female energy at the top of the stairs and wanted to share with us. As I walked closer to the house she wanted me to look inside. So I looked inside and there she was at the top of the stairs screaming, Don't touch this room."*

The house had several bedrooms upstairs, the mother's room, the father's room and the baby's room. As we slowly walked up the rickety staircase, we stopped at the top of the stairs. There in front of us was a small green door oozing with twisted mystery.

*"Don't go there, don't go there. She was brought here."* Rick said. *"They thought there was something wrong with me. I didn't like this, I didn't like this at all."* Rick started to feel dizzy as he closed his eyes as in a trance and quietly whispered, *"Who are you?"*

The house was dead silent as we all waited for the answer. *"I feel like she's trying to tell me there is an "R"* Rick said. *"Like I don't know if that is her name. But something to do with an "R" name. A real short "R" name. She's very sad. She's very, very sad."*

I probably think one of the scariest things that blew us all away was when the bedroom door slammed. I mean, there is Rick Hayes, he just started to communicate with a spirit and suddenly the door slammed so hard it came off its hinges. Something had happened in that room and we needed to find out.

We had the great pleasure to interview Joyce Wesbrooks, the great niece of Lurancy Vennum. Now in her late Eighties, she told us of her story, and her meeting of Lurancy:

*"We were not ever supposed to mention it to Aunt Rancy (Lurancy) when she visited, and we didn't. She didn't want to talk about it and be reminded of what had happened. Mother just told us that Mary Roff took over Rancy's body and that she knew things that she wouldn't ordinarily have known. I was frightened and kind of walked around her at first but we heard the story and we weren't real sure. I would think it was about possession as Lurancy went to live with the Roffs' for a time."*

Now this certainly confounded people here in Watseka. Mary had been dead for 12 years and no one expected her to return. They did test her knowledge of events as well as family affairs and personal memories. Anything they could think of. And within a few days Lurancy Vennum, or Lurancy under the power of Mary Roff, had convinced the Roff family that she was indeed their dead daughter.

It was our conclusion that Asa Roff had never reconciled himself to his daughter's death. It was about him finally coming to terms with the fact that his daughter died. It brought release to Mary's father as he had felt a lot of guilt for having to put her in an asylum. This was her way of coming back, through

Lurancy to forgive him more or less.

The story became more heart breaking for when it was time for Mary Roff to leave the body of Lurancy Vennum, the Roff's' would have to lose their daughter all over again in turn watch her die twice.

# THE STRANGE CASE OF MANTENO STATE HOSPITAL

We needed to find an asylum to correspond with the story of Mary Roff being committed. As the original Peoria Asylum was torn down we decided to utilize Manteno State Hospital in Illinois as our location. Built in 1927 and closed in 1985, the total inmates peaked around 8,000 and consisted of half male and half female. The Morgan cottage being the only building left housed upwards of two hundred and twenty people. Patients of all different types of diagnosis, from schizophrenia to manic depression and even bipolar disorders were committed. At one time in these types of asylums, you could be institutionalized for anything. If you couldn't sleep, if you had epilepsy, suffered from autism or if you masturbated too much. Over 500 phobias existed that could get you committed. You could walk in but never walk out.

At the Manteno Asylum the whole place reeked of anguish as the peeling paint was a crazed masterpiece on its own. Hundreds of patient shoes lined the flooded basement along with the mold infested hospital records. The iron security doors were excessively bent, the windows were broken and the dispelled roof revealed the night stars. In a state of disrepair all that remained was just one water therapy bathtub, which proved to be quite active with memories of torture and tears. One of the treatments in those days was the cold water baths which consisted of putting the patient into scalding hot baths, then dunking them in icy cold water. It was to shock the system in hopes that it would cure insanity.

*"At night you can sneak across to the dormitory which is considered to be the Morgan Cottage and where the windows are you can see ghostly shadows walk back and forth,"* describes paranormal investigator Rob Johnson.

We were able to catch some great EVPs and Rob's pacing shadow figures. We also captured what we believed to be a little ghost boy. Philip was in the rustic hallway filming and Keith and I were monitoring it on the Thermal Imager. The entity was right in front of Philip yet he couldn't see this child ghost at all. Philip actually walked up and touched it but there was nothing there. We had two cameras rolling, it was creepy and it moved. Reminiscent of some kind of small creature, a childlike thing. We all stood in amazement as we were not sure what to do. This capture was truly terrifying but it also was tender being that this may be a little lost soul of Manteno State Hospital.

*"As I am walking someone just told me. Mommy, Mommy. The spirit that is having me sway back and forth has the mental capacity of a small child. Someone just told me Mommy, Mommy, again,"* cried out Rick Hayes.

# THE STRANGE CASE OF GLORE PSYCHIATRIC MUSEUM

*"In those days when people would have been put into an institution, mental healthcare as we know it today didn't exist. Treatments at that time were little more than keeping the insane away from the rest of us,"* Troy Taylor from "The Possessed."

What better place to research twisted mental health care then the Glore Psychiatric Museum, home of the self-portraits of the insane. Glore Psychiatric Museum was a fascinating scary place to say the least. Located in St. Joseph, Missouri, home of Jesse James. Wikipedia quotes "it is one of the fifty most unusual museums in the United States." Its exhibits feature the 130-year history of the adjacent state mental hospital, State Lunatic Asylum No. 2 and illustrates the history of mental health treatment through the ages. The museum displays artifacts used in mental hospitals around the US. What seemed humane back in the year 1874 seems quite barbaric today.

We interviewed Kathy Reno curator of the museum as she took us on a tortured tour and filled us in with all the graphic details:

*"In the seventeenth and eighteenth centuries, mental illness was believed to be possession by evil spirits. Often the mentally ill*

*became the victims of bizarre exorcisms or casting out rituals.*
*Such as the tranquilizer chair, it was developed by Doctor*
*Benjamin Rush, the father of American psychiatry and also one of*
*the original signers of the Declaration of Independence. The chair*
*was used to calm an agitated patient. It was believed that if you*
*strapped a patient in obviously their muscles are going to relax.*
*From here doctors would administer treatment. Legs are strapped,*
*arms are strapped as they would be totally immobilized. They*
*might be in this chair for up to six months, however long it took to*
*calm down the patient."*

*"These are also trephination tools. We know that in*
*prehistoric times they were drilling holes in skulls. There's been*
*some debate in what they were trying to accomplish. But we know*
*that they were experimenting with how to heal the brain. Whether*
*a trephination drill, a copper ceremonial trephination knife or a*
*bronze stone hammer with a surrogated edge they were all used to*
*cut open the skull to cure madness. Madness was thought to be*
*possessed by demons because they didn't understand the concept of*
*epilepsy. To them, what they were accomplishing with trephination*
*was releasing the demons, whatever was disturbing this person."*

Then there was the Utica Crib, a restraint device from the
nineteenth century. The Utica Crib was named after the New York
State Lunatic Asylum at Utica. The whole concept came to
America by a French physician in 1846. The crib was made of
wood and metal with a wire bottom and slatted sides. The crib was

constructed to look like a child's crib but also had a caged roof. It was eighteen inches deep, six feet long and three feet wide so the patient could not move his legs or arms. From there they could deal with out of control patients and provide whatever therapy they deemed necessary. The particular Utica crib we saw, you could see how terribly scratched the inside was from the patients trying to claw themselves out.

# THE STRANGE CASE OF WANDA

Wanda, a homely young girl arrived at the asylum when she was just eighteen years old. Her husband had simply got tired of her and had her committed. Feeling depressed she was immediately put into a Utica crib to help stop her suicidal tendencies. There she would remain for almost forty years. After the asylum lost its funding, it was scheduled to be shut down and the broken woman was to be set free. Unable to walk due to the time spent in the crib, her legs no longer supported her failing body. Wanda was now forced to hop around like a frog. Once a lady, she now resembled a disfigured animal. Upon release she painfully lifted her hands slowly to her wrinkled face and with her dirty overgrown fingernails she clawed her eyes out.

If you were not crazy when you entered the lunatic asylum you sure was when you left. That is, if you ever left at all.


It makes you wonder who the real lunatics where in the asylum.

# THE STRANGE CASE OF ANNELIESE MICHEL

Audio excerpts of Anneliese Michel (the real Emily Rose) possession tapes were used as our diabolical sound recreations. Horrific as one would think, this audio recording lasted over one hour and could scare anyone to death. The excerpts we used were the actual recordings from that Exorcism of 1975, which sounded like six voices or demons simultaneously screaming. Hour after hour, week after week, month after month, these devious tones echoed in my head. The post process of our film, "The Possessed" would take months to complete and was beginning to get to me. I was in need of a break even if it was just for a moment, to smell the roses, look outside and feel that there was still some goodness left in the world.

*"Annaliese Michel, going back to her case, she was actually a very devout catholic. But she had an illness to the point where she had to take medication and unfortunately it opened her up to receive demonic attacks,"* states Bishop James Long.

For our film "The Possessed" we interviewed seven teenagers from ages 14-18 years old (coming of age) who had said they were possessed by the Devil. None of them had ever met, spoke or even knew about each other as they lived in different towns and states. Yet they all had similar stories. Many had gone through breakdowns, needed psychiatric help and had reached out for an Exorcism. All had lost touch and were trying to fit back in to society. They were cutters, listened to death metal music, angry and wanted to end their life. Despite of its bad wrap, the "Dark One" does not endorse Death Metal Music (For all we know he dances to Donny Osmond). Cutters are the ones who cuts to relieve themselves from emotional pain with any sharp object, such as a knife, razor, glass etc. and are generally ashamed and hide it. Mary Roff from the Watseka Wonder case was also a form of a cutter as she had done bloodletting on herself. She would take leeches and apply them to her skin complaining that she had a pain in her head that she wanted to have dissolved. Mary's love for leeches went too far to the point she had them as pets. Although her weight was only one hundred pounds, she had lost nearly all her blood.

"*In the early days of modern medicine, bleeding was actually used to try to balance the minds and the bodies of people that were either physically or mentally ill. Doctors would apply leeches to their faces, to their temples, or other parts of their bodies and the leeches would actually be allowed to drain blood from the people who were sick*" according to Troy Taylor, "The Possessed."

Leeches are still used today for medical treatment worldwide.

# THE STRANGE CASE OF THE POSSESSED

Author Steven LaChance shares with us the strange case of Helen and her daughter Kelly in this opening interview as seen in "The Possessed."

*"She was a normal child. A normal teenager. What she went through can only be classified as a possession. Kelly would stand and stare, in the middle of the night, at her parents. It was obvious by the look in her eyes, that the thoughts she was having, was to kill her family."*

*"I kept getting this feeling like I was worthless, that there was nothing left for me to do but to just kill myself,"* Kelly said.

She began cutting herself. Cuts that were meant to relieve any sort of pain that she was going through. Cuts that if she harmed herself she wouldn't have to harm her parents. Kelly tried cutting her arms and taking lots of pills. She explains:

*"I cut pretty deep. It got so bad it started scarring up my arms. I tried covering them up so no one would see them. Sometimes it was just to cut it, release it and let it out. Then sometimes it was, do it deeper, do it harder. I just started getting really mean and I didn't like nobody. I just wanted to stay in my room and listen to music. I kept wanting to stab them and hurt*

them really bad and watch them bleed. It was horrible."

"*Possession is very common with children. When they are inflicted, you never know what is actually going to come through them. You never know if it's going to be something on a negative level or if it's going to be something on a positive,*" explained John Zaffis.

Dewi Morgaine a young girl from Germany found herself waking up in bed covered in blood. She felt a connection to this story and in her broken English she agreed to talk to us.

"*I don't even remember what exactly happened. I just know there was a razor lying beside my bed. I woke up and I saw blood everywhere, on my arms and on the sheets. I cut myself with razor blades, with glass, anything that was sharp enough to make myself bleed. It was like someone or something dark was inside of me.*"

"*My mother cried when I bled and I would laugh very mean at her. It felt healthy to cut. I became obsessed with seeing my own blood. If I saw my own blood it felt satisfying. Something in me screamed that I shouldn't do it. My father came to me and said, 'Dewi, those are not your eyes..... Those eyes are the devil's eyes.'*"

Dewi now in tears, feeling broken she tells us of how it

began:

*"I was possessed when I was thirteen years old. It took a long time and it was difficult for me to breathe. I was like 'Why I can't breathe?' I had it very much of the time. My parents brought me to a medium. A very good psychic. She asked me if I had problems with breathing. 'I do, I said, actually I have a lot of problems with breathing. She then told me that it is because……. It's because you have a demon hanging around your neck.'"*

The story of Marcus's possession entailed an investigation in the local graveyard. As we interviewed both the Mother Anita and her son Marcus, it was clear that she would have done anything to save her son including taking on the demon herself.

Marcus recalls,

*"I was growling, saying things that I normally wouldn't say. You know, I was trying to be physical with people. I got this really cold feeling all over my body and I just went blank. When I came to, I had three to four bounty hunters and police holding on to me."*

His Mother Anita describes that crazy night.

*"Marcus fell down, his arms went limp and he started shaking. He was foaming at the mouth and his eyes was dilated back in his head. So I immediately thought he was having a convulsion. But when I touched him I could feel an energy, it was*

69

*like electricity coming from him."*

*"Get off of my son now, I screamed!" Come into me you bastard, come into me!" Marcus's eyes were now glowing, reddish looking as his facial features were trying to change on me. He was cussing, he lunged at me. He was literally trying to hurt me and the police was all on him trying to hold him back."*

Anita continued with her fight, *"Come out of him, I command you! As I walk through the valley of death, I shall fear no evil. Come into me, I command you. Now look at me, look at me. I fear you not."*

Anita and Marcus had worked with us on several paranormal investigations. The video footage of Marcus's possession is mind blowing but it is nothing compared to a Mother's battle to save her son.

The one most common similarity that stood out of all these cases of possession was a memory that all the victims remembered. **They all had heard rhythmic sounds of marching feet of soldiers, drums and scratching sounds.** I had read this type of description in my previous research but where? Then it dawned on me, I had read this in the real Exorcist's diary. I had been given a copy of this diary 'more like a journal' from a forensic psychiatrist and doctor of neuroscience for my studies of possession. There were only six copies known to be made with the original in the safety of the Vatican.

Below is an excerpt from the real Exorcist diary written in 1949 by Rev. Raymond Bishop. The possessed boys name is represented by the letter R.

*January 15, 1949, at the home of R in Cottage City, Maryland a dripping noise was heard by R and his Grandmother in the Grandmother's bedroom. This noise continued for a short time and then the picture of Christ on the wall shook as if the back of the wall had been thumped. By the time the parents of R returned home there was a very definite scratching sound under the floor boards near the grandmother's bed. From this night on, the scratching, was heard every night about seven o'clock and would continue until midnight. The family thought that the scratching was caused by a rodent of some kind. An exterminator was called in who placed chemicals under the floor boards, but the scratching sound continued and became more distinct when people stamped on the floor.*

*This scratching continued for ten days and then stopped. The family finally believed that the rodent had died. The boy, R seemed to think he still heard the noise but the family did not hear anything for a period of three days. When the sound became audible again, it was no longer in the upstairs bedroom but had moved downstairs to the boy's bedroom. It was heard as the sound of squeaking shoes along the bed and was heard only at night when the boy went to bed. The squeaking sound continued for six nights, and on the sixth night scratching again was audible. The mother, grandmother and boy while lying on the bed on this night heard something coming toward them similar to* **the rhythm marching feet and the beat of drums.** *The sound would travel the length of the mattress and then back and repeat this action until the mother asked"Is this you, Auntie?" (The Aunt had died in St. Louis two weeks after the first sounds were heard in the home of R). The mother continued asking questions but had no verbal reply. She asked this question, "If you are R's Auntie, knock three times." There were waves of air striking the grandmother, mother and the boy, and three distinct knocks were heard on the floor. The mother asked again, "If you are R's Auntie, tell me positively by knocking four times." Four distinct knocks were heard. Then there followed claw scratching on the mattress which* **beat out a rhythm as of marching soldiers.**

The similarity of this diary and our interviews provides truth that the sound of scratching and a military style presence is valid when it comes to possession. Possession, Exorcism and Legion are all military terms referencing, the war between good and evil. Our interviews were conducted in 2009, where the Exorcist diary was written in 1949. Both describe the victims hearing the same scratching and marching sounds. Could this be the soul's early warning to prepare us for battle against our inner demons, or could it be the sound of the Devil himself? One thing for sure is *"Something wicked this way comes."*

*"And it shall be, when thou hearest the sound of marching,*

*then thou shalt go out to battle."* American Standard Bible Version (1901)

"The Possessed" originally was   called 'Children Of The Grave 2' but since the subject matter was to do with a much darker side, possessed children, the title of the show was changed. "The Possessed" was third in the Spooked TV series to run on the Syfy Channel. Winner of best Paranormal Documentary.

# THE STRANGE CASE OF THE EXORCIST FILE

What intrigued me about this project was that "The Exorcist" was by far the scariest horror movies I had ever seen. I remember lucid nightmares after viewing it. It boldly combined sensitive subjects such as religion and the innocence of a child possessed by the devil. It was based on a true story, or true events may be a better wording. The actual case was about a boy not a girl as portrayed in the movie. Some of the things that happened in the movie happened in real life but to a boy not a girl. We went down to St. Louis to find the real people and tell the real story.

We talked to Eileen Dreyer, New York Times bestselling, award-winning author, known as Kathleen Korbel to her Silhouette readers. She has 28 romance novels published and is the great niece of the real Exorcist, Father William Bowden as portrayed by Max Von Sydow in the movie. A lovely and talented lady who agreed to be interviewed by us and held nothing back when it came to talk about her memories growing up with her great Uncle.

*"Saint Louis had the story for years. You know, it was kind of the 'best kept' secret in Saint Louis. We kind of considered the movie a comic book as opposed to what we really knew had happened. You know, there was no face makeup, there was no spinning 360 degrees. We thought that the true story should be told."*

Richard Novosak a University student of Father William Bowdern remembered,

*"When I was a high school student at St. Louis University High, Father William Bowdern was my religion teacher. A kindly old man, seemed so gentle. In fact, he didn't seem like he could even control the class, let alone a demon."*

I couldn't believe here is the scariest movie of all time and no one had ever filmed inside the real house that the possession and some of the exorcism was performed. This was the boy's uncle's house he had come to stay with when he was visiting St. Louis. For a documentarian it was a chance to find out the truth and for a paranormal investigator, it was the case of a lifetime not to mention a demonologist's dream.

We asked William B. Bradshaw who has an actual Ph.D. in Christian-Judeo Demonology what his take was on the 1949 Exorcism.

*"Whenever one thinks of religion, it's a subjective thing. Some of us believe one thing, some of us believe another. I guess that's the reason we have some many denominations, it allows us to express our own religious beliefs. So, when there's some particular religious incident, how do we know whether it's true or false? Well, as far as exorcisms are concerned that are authorized by the Roman Catholic Church, there's no question about how we*

*separate fact from fiction. Many people don't realize that with any exorcism authorized by the Roman Catholic Church, there is a written transcript required to be taken, just like in a court trial. There is a word for word written transcript and we're able to read back on that transcript to see what did or did not actually happen. In this particular incident, from everything I've heard, from all the descriptions that people have given me as to what the written transcript says, this is a real exorcism. This was a case of actual demon possession."*

The transcript William Bradshaw spoke of I soon would find out was the Exorcist Diary I had in my possession.

The Exorcist horror house was bought by a Goth rocker who purchased the home for the sole reason it was previously the Exorcist residence. He was kind enough to let us in and document our findings and reveal to the outside world what *"the scariest bedroom"* looked like. One of the scenes from the 1973 movie "The Exorcist" that has always struck a scary chord with me, was the scene when the priest would walk up to the house and ring the doorbell. Slowly the door would open and an ungodly sound from the top of the stairs would echo throughout ones soul. Well this time it was me not the priest that would recreate this walk. The first thing I did when the infamous door opened was look up at the intimidating stairway leading to the Devil Boy's room at the top of the stairs. Here I was in Lucifer's lair and there was no turning back.

The Rev. Francis X. Cleary was just twenty years old, a Jesuit Seminarian when Jesuits allegedly performed an exorcism on a 14-year-old boy in St. Louis. He had become the local historian of the infamous Exorcist case and shared his view.

*"During the day the boy would be manic and would attack a crucifix in the room. He came up here to be baptized in our church and of course Father Bowdern's exorcism. Presumably his aunt was into chatting with the devil. The aunt was involved in Ouija boards and stuff like that. "He wasn't talking to the devil, the devil was speaking through him."*

The Ouija board is a flat wooden board with the letters of the alphabet, the numbers 0–9, the words "yes", "no", "hello" (occasionally), and "goodbye", along with various symbols and graphics. It uses a planchette (small heart-shaped piece of wood or plastic) as a movable indicator to indicate the spirit's message by spelling it out on the board during a séance. Participants place their fingers on the planchette, and it is moved about the board to spell out words by possible spirits.

Can you believe it?, I actually went out and bought a real 1949 Ouija board that one of our team members Sandra Oates found on Craig's List. An exact duplicate to the one that the haunted boy and his Aunt would have used. It was used as a prop in our documentary, "The Exorcist File" despite how dangerous it could be. I remember flying back to Los Angeles with the thought of taking it with me. Whether I believed in its magic or not, I didn't want to take any chances so I had it shipped to my house. There was no way I was traveling on the plane with it. I had researched too many cases about these boards of doom.

We interviewed a teenage girl in the Midwest who told us how she and her friends would sneak out at night and use an Ouija board at the cemetery. They would try and summon up serial killers such as Ted Bundy, Ed Gein and John Wayne Gacy. It was just a big game to them until the board answered back by spelling out the name, "Pogo." John Wayne Gacy was a convicted serial killer and rapist who sexually assaulted and murdered at least 33 people in Chicago, Illinois. Gacy was also known as the "Killer Clown" in which he named "Pogo" as he would dress up as a circus clown at parades and children's parties.

Soon after that the girl complained about hearing scratching sounds and being attacked in her bed at night. She heard voices and openly spoke of a little dead girl that would visit her. She believed in the devil but not in God. Personally if you believe in one, you have to believe in the other. It's like believing in bad but not good, death but not life or hate but not love. There are always two sides of the coin, heads or tails. You need to have an opposite to justify a contrast, a state of being strikingly different from something else. A reverse choice to know which path you should follow, up or down. Both must exist to realize there's a difference between. Even messing with an Ouija board can go either way, Yes or No.

Was it the use of the Ouija board that opened up the Exorcist boy to possession? It was later said that the boy was not mentally sound due to sexual abuse possibly by his aunt. My research has shown that his aunt had MS (Multiple Sclerosis) and was pretty much bed ridden. She could hardly move so how would that be possible? The sexual abuse allegations also pointed to the church as the boys experience is documented in the Exorcist's diary.

*"Brother Emmet was escorting R back to the basement floor of the Hospital when R went into a fighting spell. The Brother was alone and shouted for help, but it was some time before the other Brothers heard him. Brother Emmet was quite exhausted from the struggle. R was carried into the entrance and placed into his fifth floor room. The Fathers immediately began the prayers of exorcism, and the usual indications of violence continued. The devil showed his power again by saying that he would have R awaken and ask for a knife. He had threatened to kill those who molested him while in his seizure. When R came out of the spell, he asked for a knife so that he might cut an Easter egg. A little later the devil said that he would have R awaken and ask for a drink of water, and R carried out the plan."*

A follow up to the Midwest Ouija board case revealed that the teenage girl had passed due to cancer. No one really knew as the family had now disappeared. There was also some talk about her

79

being on heavy meds and acting crazy as well as appearing on a Jerry Springer type show right after our interview.

This case was definitely getting to me. Between the conflicting stories, the demonology research and then reading the actual diary of "The Exorcist," I was mentally exhausted. Dark visions were becoming quite clear. Being somewhat of an Empath, negative things around you have a tendency to take you down. One can only help someone wanting to be helped. It was my hope she was safe and at peace.

The evidence we had captured on our investigation at the Exorcist house was quite overbearing. Vulgar and violent EVPs has always been a force to reckon with. Whether the entity uses the F or the C word you know you are in for one hell of a ride. We had captured several foul words that night. We also caught a black mass on video, extreme cold spots on our temp units and even one of the paranormal investigators, Greg Myers got severely attacked. While Greg was being filmed during an EVP session he complained of a burning sensation around his neck area. With Keith Age on thermal, Sandra Oates on audio and Philip Booth on camera we caught a shape of a cross appearing or should I say burning into his neck. Vicki Main was our Sensitive Medium along with Dr. Michael Lynch from Para-Vision. It was an intense investigation that none of us would ever forget.

It was time to gather up all of our notes and evidence and leave St. Louis ("THANK GOD!") and head back to Los Angeles and assemble this puppy.

# THE STRANGE CASE OF THE EXORCIST FILE II

Being back in LA, I never knew for sure if I had brought something home with me or not. Did I pick up a dark hitch hiker that night of The Exorcist house investigation or was I just being para-noid?

It was always in the back of my mind as I had heard many stories of spirit attachments. There are many forms, but Dark Beings or NEA (Negative Energy Attachments) are the worst. They are more dangerous than any haunted location as you yourself become haunted. Whether through Satanic ritual, use of an Ouija board or simply playing with the dark side, you need to protect yourself. Spiritual protection is based on personal and religious beliefs.

Throughout the editing process of "The Exorcist File," I remember seeing strange shadows. The show in general carried a heavy vibe so I decided not to take a chance. I had my 3 year old son Gabriel stay with his Mother (now my ex-wife) in Indiana until the show was complete.

With the help of research investigators Greg Myers and Sandy Oates who without their dedication we could not bring this story to the screen. We focused on the untold story, the human elements as well as the nonhuman. We found out things that would help put backbone to the story or could distinguish it in seconds.

Arnold Spirtas who runs Spirtas Wrecking Company is St. Louis's eyesore remover. He's the man you call when you want the past destroyed, whether it's a building or demon infested furniture. It was Arnold's job now to pull down the old Grand Manor, a nursing home along with all its belongings including "The Exorcist" furniture. Arnold explains:

*"They were telling me that the furniture from the actual exorcism was brought to the Grand Manor from the old Alexian Brothers' Hospital and it was stored on the fourth floor. It was kind of locked up in the rooms and needs to be removed." They said, "Well, it's a very, very sensitive issue for us. It was religious and well, we think it's spooked!" I said, "How do you mean, spooked?" They said, "Exactly what I'm saying. Spooked! Things happen when you're around it."*

Arnold and his deconstruction team, along with a priest who blessed the wrecking ball. Tore down The Grand Manor Nursing Home and all of its furniture. That was the end of that, so we thought. We ended up finding "The Exorcist" furniture locked up in cold storage on an air force base somewhere in Illinois.

Reading "The Exorcist Diary" we were privy to all kind of new information. For instance, the boy's uncle would fasten large sheets of wrapping paper to the bed. Apparently when the boy went into a fit of possession, he would draw and write things, things that the devil told him to. In the morning the priests would remove the paper and study them back at the church.

The following is an excerpt taken from the Exorcist diary.

*1). In answer to the first set of questions he wrote the Roman numeral X. (It was clearly the numeral, with crossbars at top and bottom). This was written four times on this first occasion and was repeated several times during the exorcism, usually in answer to the question, "diem."*

*2). I will stay 10 days and return after the 4 days are up.*

*3). I am the devil himself. You will have to pray for a month in the Catholic Church.*

*4). In answer to the command to give ("Nomen lingua Latina.") I speak the language of the persons. (Word language was misspelled). I will put in R's mind when he makes up his mind that the Priests (sic) are wrong about writing English. I will, that is the English. I will, that is the devil will try to get his mother and dad to hate the Catholic Church. I will answer to the name of Spite.*

*5). In 10 days I will give a sign on his chest he will have to have it covered to show my power.*

*6). He drew a strange thing that looked somewhat like a map, with*

*"2,000 ft." written on it (apparently connected with early dreams about hidden treasure and a map to find it). I believe that it was in this connection that he spoke also, saying, "Yeah, this is what I got on the Ouija board." He drew a face also, and wrote the words: "Dead Bishop."*

Father Raymond Bishop was the authorized priest in charge of assembling the writings from 14 other priests, creating "The Exorcist Diary."

Later on Father Raymond Bishop would die tragically.

My long talks with demonologist, William B. Bradshaw helped me understand the churches stance on evil as I have always believed in God but was never an avid church goer. I had told him before our interview, if there was any question to sensitive too answer, just say *"No comment."* It now intrigued me to see which questions he would adapt that answer too. There were quite a few.

He moved on to explain to me the meaning of possession and how one becomes possessed. Below is my interpretation. *Everything God knows his right hand Angel knows. They both know if a certain man or woman are destined to be a great help to human kind. After Lucifer's fall, it was this Fallen Angel's mission to stop all good Samaritans by causing distractions along their way. Those distractions could be alcohol, drugs, greed, jealousy etc. This is how the devil would be able to possess you, the divine,*

84

*by diverting your attention away from the (peace) prize. Alcohol gets you drunk, and you get addicted with drugs. This leads to disease, prison, murder and finally loss of life. Selfishness, injustice, lack of compassion, vanity to name a few are the devils testing grounds. All these paths lead love to hate, life to death and good to evil. The devil simply owns you when you give up your chance to righteousness. Stripped of love you are a just a possession, possessed by the King of Darkness himself.*

When we live our life to the fullest potential, obstacles cannot get in our way. For we are precise, a beautiful driven spirit that will stay the course. It's okay to get lost as long as we are found. Every morning when you wake, make it your soul mission to be who you are meant to be. Everyone dies but not everyone lives.

*In memory of Rev. Francis X. Cleary*

Choosing locations on where to shoot our Exorcist File documentary was very important. We had the real house, graveyard and churches locked down but where would we film our recreation of the infamous exorcism scene. The original exorcism took place back in 1949 at the old Alexian Brothers Hospital in St. Louis, Missouri. Since then they had torn down the fifth floor, where it actually happened, and remodeled the hospital without. I'm not a big fan of cheesy reenactments so this exorcism had to be as real as it can get. We needed a real spooky hospital or asylum as a Hollywood set would not do.

# THE STRANGE CASE OF THE QUEEN MARY

A few years back I attended a para convention at the haunted Queen Mary in Long Beach, California. *Case in point this city is where Watseka Wonders Lurancy Vennum is buried.* I think that convention was the second to last time we saw our dear friend and publicist Donn Shy. A beautiful soul, may she rest in peace. "The Queen Mary" or "The Grey Ghost" as it was called is a retired ocean liner that sailed primarily on the North Atlantic Ocean from 1936 to 1967, and it is extremely haunted. Though the search for Jackie the drowned little girl in the pool area was our main focus, the bow of the old ship was extremely active that night. Darkness Radio's Dave Shrader hosted the event yet Chris Fleming had taken lead on the paranormal investigation and had gotten some Class A results. Chris had captured some real-time EVPs that were of German dialect.

It always perplexed me how some paranormal investigators that travel abroad, for example to Dracula's Castle in Romania or Frankenstein's Castle in Germany, do an EVP session while asking questions in English. What's even more frustrating is when their so called ghosts answer them back in English. Unless 'Rosetta Stone' exists in the afterlife it makes no sense to me at all. If it was indeed the ghosts of Dracula's Castle speaking, they would communicate in their own foreign tongue. After all, what we are in life we are in death and that would include the language we speak. While filming

"Soul Catcher," our Native American ghost story we had gotten EVPs that were in Apache and Arapaho. In "Children Of The Grave", one of the orphanage locations we used, POWs were said to be locked up in the tunnels during WWI and we did get several EVPs in German.

During the Queen Mary convention I met the future owner of Rolling Hills Asylum, Sharon Coyle who at that time had no idea at all she was going to own a haunted asylum. Visiting her in Bethany, New York a few years later, after she bought Rolling Hills Asylum, I expected to see a mad caretaker, frozen in the snow. *"All work and no play makes Sharon a dull girl?"* That was not the case at all. Sharon was full of excitement, a dedicated and passionate owner. She was kind enough to unlock the asylum doors and let us shoot our recreations of the most infamous exorcisms of all time.

*In memory of Donn Shy*

# THE STRANGE CASE OF ROLLING HILLS ASYLUM

Rolling Hills Asylum, originally The Genesee County Poor Farm of 1826. A poor farm is a facility that houses orphans, widowed women, poor, mentally ill and minor criminals. Rolling Hills is also known to be extremely haunted with the ghosts of past inmates, including children spirits and a seven foot giant named Roy. Staff members have reported hearing, screams, children laughing, doors slamming and being touched. Full body apparitions, shadow people, light abnormalities and EVPs is just some of the documented paranormal evidence captured here.

Bethany New York, and it was ten degrees outside. After scouting the location we chose the room at the top of Rolling Hills Asylum to be our stage. It had a large round Gothic window in the center and plenty of room for our cameras and dolly track. We also were able to find an original hospital wire bed amongst other real artifacts that were hidden in the basement. Our set was now dressed with historical props and set pieces. It was time to exorcise. The actors were cast, the lights were placed and the cameras started rolling. Action…

Suddenly the Asylum room doors started to shake violently. What on earth was that? We stopped the cameras and I went off to search for what was causing the disruption. Into the hallway I ventured, there ahead where the guilty old doors that was shaking. I opened them one by one as I entered into each room and closed the doors behind me. There I stood quietly as I looked around, checking for any sign of draft or broken windows. I held my breath and listened deeply for any movement. There was no draft or outside wind at all. All the windows remained in tacked and unbroken. The doors were a little warped due to age but seemed sturdy and level. It made no logical sense why the doors would shake like that. After no success of figuring this mystery out, I returned back to set.

Take 2, the actors where on their marks as we start to roll the exorcism reenactment once again. We didn't even make it five minutes into the scene when the doors started shaking again. We stopped and I went off to search one more time to see what was going on. I still could not find any reason why the doors would shake every time we did the exorcism scene. At that point it was getting dark and we were losing our light so we decided to film (MOS) without sound. We could always add ADR (additional dialogue recording) later at the studio. That was just the beginning of our crazy experiences at Rolling Hills Asylum. We never did find out what caused the doors to shake violently that night of our filming of "The Exorcist File." But it was just the extra touch we needed to complete our demon documentary.

"The Exorcist File - Haunted Boy" went on to be a top rental in Redbox of July of 2014. Winner of Best Feature Film / Nashville Horror Film Festival. Now available on iTunes.

# THE STRANGE CASE OF THE MAYFAIR HOTEL

The night of our St. Louis theatrical premiere of, "The Exorcist File," I decided to stay at the downtown historic Mayfair hotel built in 1924. Noted guests of the hotel throughout the years were Irving Berlin, John Barrymore, Douglas Fairbanks, Cary Grant, Harry Truman and Lyndon B. Johnson. It was a seedy old place but with our film premiering at the classic Tivoli Theater, within a few days, we needed a hotel quickly. St. Louis was not unfamiliar with the story of "The Exorcist" as this is where it happened. The whole town was excited to see our rendition of this untold story as both theatrical shows quickly sold out.

Most of the film's paranormal cast attended including Eileen Dreyer, Keith Age, William Bradshaw our demonologist, Nick (the house owner) and Arnold the wrecking baller. After an exhausting premiere and after-party at the local nightclub it was time to call it a night.

I got back to the hotel around 1AM. As I waited in the retro lobby for the vintage elevator to take me up to the 4th floor, I couldn't help but notice how spooky this place was. The hotel resembled the hotel in the movie '1408' with John Cusak. If you haven't seen it I recommend you do. The way the ghosts are portrayed is the perfect interpretation of how a residual haunting would play out. Even my hotel room 408 had the exact layout to

90

Cusak's room including the funky bathtub. I have to laugh when I watch that movie as for even the paranormal book signing scene seems spot on. (Golf clap)

After a quick bath, it was time to get some sleep. As I started to drift off, I could feel the sheets slowly being pulled off the bed. Illuminated only by the downtown streetlights, I could see a large shadow creature hovering over me. It had the appearance of tall man with strange stubby horns. Horns that looked like they were cut off or filed down. Suddenly I felt my foot grabbed from the bottom of the mattress as I was forcefully dragged to the ground. I quickly crawled across the hotel floor to the nightstand and turned on the old lamp. As the bulb lit up the room, the shadow figure dissipated. Still in shock I looked down and that's when I saw, red claw marks, scratched across my foot. The same foot I was pulled out of bed with. I franticly limped into the next room to get my night vision camera for at this point if I was going to be brutally murdered I was going to document it. I calmed myself down, got back on the bed and waited for this things next move.

Nothing happened again that dark night but you can bet I checked out the very next morning. On my way out of the hotel I stopped by the front desk to drop off the key, which in this case was a real key not a plastic card with a pizza ad. I said to the hotel desk clerk *"Do you know if my room is haunted?"* Before I could even finish my sentence or tell her my room number, she said *"Yes, 408 right? We have had numerous reports. Legend has it, back in the day when prohibition was in place, there was a lot of bootlegging going on in St. Louis. One night there was a big party up on the fourth floor and several people were murdered in that room, killed by gangsters. The room is haunted sir"*

Limping out the lobby door I turned and casually screamed, *"You think?"*

That terrifying night still haunts me today.

# THE STRANGE CASE OF SEX WITH GHOSTS

Amidst dark hours we were called in to help a married couple who was complaining about being sexually violated by an unseen force. They were in their late thirties and had two children. The family lived in a beautiful rural home on the outskirts of Nashville, Tennessee in which they had just moved into. Being that there were children involved this would be an extra-sensitive case. We definitely needed to bring in a priest who was also an Exorcist so we asked our dear friend Bishop James Long to accompany us on this roller coaster to hell.

Bishop James Long is currently the Archbishop for the United States Old Catholic Church and offers Spiritual and Life help for those who seek assistance. He also is an Exorcist who has performed over 27 exorcisms to date.

When we arrived there seemed to be a questionable feeling of disarray in the house. The children seemed drained and their parents was in a zombie like state. We set up for the parents interviews to be followed by a blessing of the house. The blessing was to be conducted by Bishop James Long. As he explained to us one does not perform an exorcism on a house but a blessing instead. Exorcisms are done on demonic forces. It is performed by prayer, holy water and the burning of incense. This is interpreted by the Roman Catholic Church as a purification ritual.

The Mother went on to explain: "*I would be lying down in bed when suddenly I felt something molesting me. I could feel the weight of a body on top of me. As I struggled, I felt my legs spread apart.*" She then looked to her husband that was sitting next to her, and said "*and then it starting attacking my husband.*" A tear rolled down her face, her voice started to choke up as she continued. "*I would come home late at night, you see I worked the graveyard shift. When I got home I found my husband on the bed, he would be getting oral sex. I could see his erection and the movement of lips on his manhood, but there was no one there. It was like some kind of invisible force, satisfying him.*" This went on for weeks to the point that both the couple engaged in spectral sex. They started to enjoy and even look forward to the violation.

Through my research I have found this is to be classified as Incubus and Succubus attacks also known as Spectrophilia.

"*Spectrophilia is sexual attraction to ghosts or sexual arousal from images in mirrors, also the phenomenon of sexual encounters between ghosts and humans. Folklore has it that the succubus is a demon who changes into female human form to seduce men into intercourse. The succubus is said to take semen from the male for use in impregnating a woman. The incubus is a demon that is said to take on a male human form to seduce women leading to intercourse and then implanting there demon seed.*"

There are two types of individuals when it comes to spectral sex. There are people who are sexually attacked, raped and they seek help in getting rid of these dark entities. Then there are people that actually welcome these demons advances. Yes, there are people who actually enjoy ghostly sexual encounters and will provoke, even attempt to seduce these spirits.

In 2001 BBC news reported, residents of the Zanzibar Islands are in fear over a sexually voracious ghost that would attack people while they sleep in their beds at night. The ghost goes by the name of *Popo Bawa* who is said to have sodomized its victims, most of whom are men. People claim his presence is revealed by an unpleasant smell and a puff of smoke. Victims then speak of being in a trance or dreamlike state as they are molested. A previous ghost, known for attacking children, was reported to have terrorized the islands for six months.

A few years back it was pop superstar Ke$ha. In a 2012 radio interview with Ryan Seacrest, Ke$ha talked about "having sex with a ghost."

People who are visited by these spectral predators rarely ever report these attacks. Either they are scared, too embarrassed to talk about it or they enjoy these ghostly bedroom visits. More and more cases of sex with ghosts are on the rampage. Some of these victims may be looking for their 15 minutes of fame where others simply suffer from sleep disorders or night terrors (Old Hag Syndrome). No one knows for sure why these terrors occur. Studies have found that they run in families that have a genetic component. Set off by either emotional tension or the use of alcohol or drugs, they have also been linked to mental disorders.

Imaginary lovers have a tendency to screw with your head more than screw with anything else. The more we began to uncover from this Nashville attack, the more this couple wanted to bury. It would seem we opened up a big can of demon-worms. Apparently the Mother was also delving into witchcraft. The house was infested with books on black magic and fallen angels. She was practicing the art of dark magic and knew all the demons names like the back of her hand.

Never call a demon by its name for you might just be opening up a doorway, an invitation to the foul to come visit. For instance, if I called out your name, would you not acknowledge my request and even answer back? In most cases, I think you would. So why in hell would one call out a demons name and risk the chance of inviting it in? Obviously somebody in this house had done just that. Demon names were found written all over the house. The youngest of the couple's children told me, he knew their names and had been hiding from one of them. I asked him what this demon was trying to do. He said he wasn't sure but its name began with D. Please don't say the name I thought to myself as the child began to write on the fridge with a broken crayon. He wrote the letter D, scribbled the letter A and stopped. With a nervous voice and tears in his eyes, he turned to me and asked, "*How do you spell DANGEROUS?*" It was obviously the child was scared to death.

But exactly what of?

Since the success of popular paranormal TV shows, demons has been pushed down our throats. We definitely did not want to go down that road, at least until we had some kind of legitimate proof that this indeed was a real case of demon infestation. We had come here to this house to document a said, poltergeist, incubus and succubus attack but so far, all we were finding were human related incidents rather than paranormal. As we walked through the house we had noticed a hand gun laying on the kitchen table. It appeared to be unloaded but still dangerous being that there were children nearby. Things didn't seem to add up. There was more going on here then we were being told.

The master bedroom was full of taxidermy, over a dozen deer heads with antlers were mounted on the walls. It felt very creepy as their bulging eyes seem to follow me. It was obvious that the man of the house was a hunter and an avid gun owner by the gun safe he had in the corner. I could feel the husband, now right behind me as he entered this bedroom of death.

*" I wish I knew the combination to the safe," he whispered as he began to tell me how his wife recently changed the safe's combination as she was afraid he might kill his family. The plot thickened. It was time for a team discussion and a well-deserved smoke break. We politely excused ourselves and went outside to talk. Between our puffs we couldn't help but think, "The worst is yet to come."*

After one cigarette down, I lit another. This discussion was definitely a two cigarette job. Before we head back into this estranged house we will need to discuss what's best for the family. We would need definite proof, either way. Was this a case of demons or just an act of bad parenting? Getting our thoughts and equipment together, our second wind blew in, it was time to bless the house.

It was getting late so we decided to split up. Each team member would investigate a different part of the house while Bishop James Long started his cleansing by blessing the exterior first. If this residence had something evil inside, the idea was to trap it by blessing the outside doorways first so it could not escape. Then James would perform a prayer on each room to banish the demons presence. I immediately was drawn back to the master bedroom. For me that was where the darkness dwelled. It still creeped me out all those trophy eyes watching my every move but my gut feeling would reveal I was right soon enough.

Previous case studies showed sexual attacks from entities, involved families unearthing ancient artifacts, such as arrow heads, pottery and bones. Mix that with Hoodoo or Black Magic and one just might open a realm. The reason I mention this is due to the high count of antlers found in the father's room. This could indeed amplify any dark energy, intensifying it to a sexual attack. Antlers are the animal's weapon much like the husband's guns. Evolution of antlers is sexual selection, male to male competition and a female mate choice. Deer Antler is a popular aphrodisiac. These antlers or bones can be used in spell casting to draw out its energy to invoke its spirit into another. Something was unleashed whether by magic or extreme haunting and this dead game park was feeding the situation.

Meanwhile, Keith Age had placed several audio recorders as well as the Paranormal Puck system in the master bedroom. Like the Ovilus, the Puck runs on environmental sensors but is attached to a computer usually a laptop instead of a hand held unit. You can see the changes in those sensors as the environment conditions change. Using the ITC mode (Instrumental Trans Communication), a term used to describe devices that use an electronic or mechanical means to allow spirit communication. When there are changes in the ECM (Environmental Communications Mode) or the EMF (Electronic Magnetic Field) it is translated into words in which the investigator hopes are answers to questions typed via a computer keyboard. A library of about 1000 words existed on our unit. We found the higher the reading, the more intense word the Puck would speak.

Developed by Digital Dowsing as an entertainment device, I took it with a grain of salt. Being somewhat of a skeptic I walked over to the device and typed in my first question, *"Who is the entity in this house?"* As I waited I noticed the EMF level spike, nothing could prepare me for the answer I was about to receive. The Puck answered, *"Leave ......Chris!"* Thank God I had recorded the whole thing on video to document this event as you could hear me on the recording say *"I'm outta here!"* Oh my God, the first time I attempt to use a paranormal talking gadget and this is what I get? I mean what are the odds? There was nothing normal about this para-normal activity.

Meanwhile, Bishop James Long had been quite busy blessing the other rooms in the house. Leaving the master bedroom for last, the entity would have no other choice but to be trapped here with us. With holy water in one hand, and a bible in the other. Armed with an Exorcist's prayer, James was ready for the fight of his life.

I showed Keith what I had previously received on the Paranormal Puck. A little skeptical, he went on to type a few questions of his own. Bishop Long commenced with the blessing. God's favor and protection was starting to shake things as the room went dark. Bishop Long had asked me not to film his final blessing.

*"Turn your camera off,"* he said. *"Out of respect to the victims, the distraction may also weaken the effects of the ritual against the evil spirits."* Lets not give them fame.


Suddenly the Paranormal Puck spoke again, this time it answered the question I had originally typed in, *"Who is the entity in this house?"* It answered *"LEGION!"*

"Legion" is a group of demons referred to in the Christian Bible. The Gospel of Mark, 5:9 from the King James Bible describes the following; *"And He (Jesus) asked him (the possessed man), "What is thy name?" And he answered, saying, "My name is Legion: for we are many."*

The dormant holy water that Bishop James cast moved like liquid mercury across the bed as these blessed droplets formed together like an invincible shield. The Bishops prayer echoed throughout the house as he collapsed to the floor. Exhausted and now fragile he looked up at me and smiled. The blessing was complete and the entity was no more.

The house was now clean, the blessing was successful. Monthly follow ups with the house owners proved to have no more dark activity dwelling within. It was a tough case. But at the end of the day we were glad to help. This case proved to be both fascinating and twisted with stories of sexual ghostly attacks and poltergeist encounters. How could one not be intrigued? My mind was racing for answers and I decided to dig deeper on this phenomenon.

There are more cases like this every day. But sometimes you have to involve the authorities, as human nature is at fault. It seems like Demons get blamed for everything, right? In one hundred percent of demon and possession cases, 10% are valid. The remaining 90% are usually people that are mentally unsound. But keep in mind, it doesn't really matter if you are possessed or not. If the victim truly believes they are inhabited by the devil then an exorcism will most likely work. If you believe in God it makes sense you should believe in the Devil. Remember balance is everything and opposites attract. Hot and Cold, Air and Water, Love and Hate. With the devil out there, the business of God is good.

# THE STRANGE CASE OF THE ENTITY

Having the pleasure to interview parapsychologist Dr. Barry Taff for our upcoming documentary regarding the infamous "Entity" case. The Entity is a 1982 horror film from the novel by Frank De Felitta. Based on the true story of Doris Bither in the mid-seventies, it stars Barbara Hershey as a woman tormented via "spectral rape" by an invisible entity. Excerpts from that interview are below.

Christopher: *You are a parapsychologist? What is that exactly?*

Barry: *A parapsychologist is a scientist from one of many different disciplines who studies the field of the paranormal in a scientific way. My approach is a medical approach, is a neurophysiological approach, and is an environmental approach. We measure environments, we have people take tests, we have them go through measurements, and we look at their psychological background. And Doris' background back then is not one that would play out well in the psychiatric community. She was a very, let's say troubled lady from the get go, she bounced from man to man like a ball. The problem with this is, looking at it from a Gestalt perspective, the whole, we can't ignore the possibility that some of this might have been livid fantasies played out in a way we can't explain. The energies were there in such a way that she was able to make use of them.*

*In this field of research we call such people, people who phenomena hovers around and moves with them, we call them poltergeist agents. The majority of these people that we've investigated, in my case for 42 years now, tend to be seizure prone or suffer from temporal lobe epilepsy. When they take their medication, their seizures go away, as do much of the psychokinetic manifestations. The phenomenon is real, but at the root of it may be a living, breathing psyche that's somehow using the environment to produce these events. As to whether there's more, discarnate intelligence, ghosts, maybe, maybe not, although I know this - what we saw in Doris' bedroom in the summer of 1974, was not photogenic. Yet 25 people saw the same thing at the same time. In science, in reality, there is no such thing as a mass hallucination. There's mass hysteria, but there is NOT mass hallucination. If 25 people were made to hallucinate that were collectively observing something, there would be major differences from one person to the next. That didn't exist here. We all saw the same thing at the same time.*

Christopher: *So do you believe she was raped by a ghost?*

Barry: *I believe something did attack Doris Bither because her kids, the boys, witnessed it on more than one occasion. They saw their mother, a diminutive woman, thrown around like a rag doll, and at one point, her eldest son went to help her and he was picked* up and thrown to the wall like a rag doll. The case continued to evolve. As Doris spoke more freely about her sexual encounters with the ghost, she told us there were three male entities that attacked her. Two would hold her down and one would enter her.

Christopher: *I mean it's very disturbing to think that she was being held down by two other entities and being sexually molested by another. I mean, wasn't that a shocking evaluation?*

Barry: *Doris' perception of what happened to her, Doris' belief as to what happened to her didn't play out in terms of the way we evaluated it. We couldn't prove what she was saying, nor could we disprove it. However, my training was in psychophysiology, the brain, the body behavior, and it was a little too coincidental she had three male children, all from different men, whom she had an extremely volatile, chaotic relationship with.*

*From this point on the case, it's escalated dramatically. We began seeing strange lights flying around the house at night. They'd looked like giant comets, jellied lightning, green, always lime green in color, madly flying about the rooms. We then sealed the house off from all external lighting and we still saw the lights. We began taking photographs and some of them depicted things that we never saw. What we did see, for the most part, did not photograph, which is impossible, that's an enigma. That's a paradox.*

Christopher: *First of all, it seemed that this Doris, she got off on it. Did you feel that she was getting into this ghost that was repeatedly raping her?*

Barry: *While Doris was certainly traumatized by what had happened to her, there came a point at which she seemed to actually enjoy it, as if she were having orgasms and she in fact conveyed this to Frank DiFelitta, who eventually wrote the book and the screenplay for the movie "The Entity." She never told this to us because she thought that as we were academics and we were dealing in parapsychology, not in entertainment, it wouldn't be a good thing to let other people know that she was being raped by anything or anyone.*

I have been involved with a few cases where they were not paranormal at all. When you are dealing with energy, I have found that there is no good energy or bad energy it's just energy. We interpret it as being good or bad as our senses pick up event leftovers. Residual like a scent or a stain that is hard to get out. You must leave your ego and judgment at the door and understand this is their world you are visiting.

I have found on many occasions that our paranormal devices has given us clues that this was not a paranormal event at all but a human event. Such ITC readings included words like, molest, rape, incest etc. The lack of paranormal activity combined with common sense showed that this was not a ghost attack but simply crimes committed by humans. This is a case for the authorities, CPS not the Ghostbusters. The problem being is, how do you explain this?

*"Officer, I went into this house that was infested by said demons and found out it was just the family committing abominations. And the reason I know this is my ghost gear told me so."* - EPIC FAIL-

# THE STRANGE CASE OF CHILDREN OF THE GRAVE II

We wanted to do our next project a little different. There was a lot of bullying going on out there, making national news. We thought it was important to address this issue and adapt this into our new show.

I had heard the story, the legend of Zeke the monkey face boy who was known to haunt the Lemp Mansion in St. Louis, Missouri. The Lemp Mansion was built in 1860 and then purchased by William J. Lemp (owner of Lemp Brewery) as a residence and auxiliary brewery office. It was also known as a home of numerous suicides.

The story goes that this poor boy Zeke was deformed. He actually suffered from Down's Syndrome. In the early nineteen hundreds such a disease was extremely misunderstood. Hidden by his family in disgrace this poor boy would peek out of the attic window and watch the passersby. One late night running through attic he fell down the stairs and died.

The voice of Zeke in our documentary would be important. Who would tell his story with the emotion and passion it demanded. During a Mid-South Paranormal Convention, hosted by Keith Age and his team the LGHS (Louisville Ghost Hunters

Society). I had met a young boy named Russell Stum who was suffering from a disease called Neurofibromatosis, a genetic disorder that disturbs cell growth in the nervous system, causing tumors to form on nerve tissue. It is sometimes confused with Elephantiasis. Known as The Elephant Man, John Merrick disease (a sad case indeed). Russell is a delightful chap full of spirit and I told him about Zeke. I asked him if he would like to tell his story. Russell had a fascination with the paranormal and wanted to go on an investigation so he was quite intrigued. Who better then to tell the story of an outcast then one who may be suffering himself from the same feelings?

So we headed out to the Lemp Mansion where we went on a preliminary tour of the house. It had an overwhelming dark overtone with much oppression and anger. Our main focus was Zeke and his tender story so we set up our thermal imagers in the stairwell to the attic. This was the spot his little spirit was known to roam. Philip and I were joined by paranormal investigators Anita Spiritchaser, Keith Age and equipment specialist Bill Chappell. Betsy Belanger docent of the Lemp Mansion filled us in with the history and the hauntings. Not expecting to capture any paranormal activity that night we were quite surprised.

Anita had camped out on the stairs as we set our cameras on her and the surrounding area. We could feel a cold damp draft blow by us as Anita shouted, *"Is there anybody beside me?"* She had felt a presence of the unknown and it was starting to make her nervous. Keith aimed his Thermal Imager directly to where she was sitting. The air was musty as the attic had not been opened for a long time. There were scratch and scuff marks on the old attic floor and steps rumored to be those of Zeke's feet pacing back and forth. The cold stairs of the attic illuminated with energy of a time when special children were hidden, misunderstood and locked away. One can only imagine the torment of this different little one who was dead to the world. It was our hope we could help tell his story and let him know he is loved and not forgotten.

The energy was strong that night as an eerie mist appeared in front of our cameras. The mist formed into a shape of a face, but a face covered by an old canvas sack. It had two eye holes peering through the old burlap bag which was tight over the apparition's head. The shocking part was it seemed to have an impression of a deformed face as it turned sideways. Expressions of wanting, needing almost as it was calling out from limbo, searching for the way home. Only the thermal camera was able to pick up the mists imprints, so our video cameras were locked on the Thermal Imager recording its every frame.

Anita was still sitting on the attic steps confirmed that she was experiencing a presence around her and whatever it was, it was now pulling her hair. As much as it was frightening, we couldn't run away, we were hypnotized by its ghostly movements and interactions. Betsy had placed a small teddy bear as a gift to Zeke.

*"What a beautiful boy! What a beautiful boy! Don't be*

*afraid. It's okay to move on, go to the light,"* Betsy cried.

We encouraged the little ones energy to move on, move on to the light. Just as he appeared he disappeared back into the darkness of the Lemp Mansion but this time we hoped Zeke had found his way home and moved on to the light.

Ashmore Estates now owned by the charming Robbin Terry, is a former almshouse, once part of the Coles County Poor Farm. An almshouse also known as a poor house or poor farm is a place where poor people were allowed to live for free or in exchange for work around the property. Ashmore was built in 1916 and operated until 1959, when it was purchased by Ashmore Estates, Inc. for use as a private psychiatric care facility. Ashmore Estates closed in 1987 and stood abandoned until 2006, when it was opened as a commercial haunted house. Haunted by several ghosts such as Joe who was said to die by a train accident and Elva Skinner, who died in a fire in the original almshouse.

Ashmore Estates, located along the north side of Illinois Route 16 just west of Ashmore. Hooked on Ashmore Estates from the moment we saw the three-story brick building looming in the countryside, we couldn't wait to get inside. Taken from a news article in the Journal Gazette/Times Courier by Rob Stroud, we describe our ghostly encounter.

*"Pulling up was incredible; seeing this place for the first time,* Philip Booth marveled. *"We filmed footage inside the*

*purportedly haunted 93-year-old building, built as a part of the county poor farm and now used as a haunted house."*

*"We are looking forward to going through as guests this time instead of filmmakers,"* Philip Booth said as he sat in one of the building's gloomy corridors.

*"The last time we were at Ashmore Estates we recorded sounds and images, with the help of a thermal camera, we feel are indications of the building being haunted. Our production crew, all skeptics, were mystified by some of the unexplained technical malfunctions that occurred."*

In addition, Philip said he was disconcerted when his camera was aggressively jerked from his hands three times by some unseen force. *"I don't like that feeling,"* Philip said. Christopher Booth said *"They are fascinated to think of all the indigent people, both young and old, that were sent to live and work at Ashmore Estates, isolated amidst the farm fields."*

*"Many of the grand old buildings throughout the United States that are thought to be haunted are being demolished because no one wants to maintain them"* Christopher Booth said. He praised Scott Kelley for watching over Ashmore Estates and opening it to the public.

Nathaniel West reports from the Journal Gazette/Times

Courier. ASHMORE — *"There are few occupations in which thunderstorms complete the ideal job site. Tornado chasers and Weather Channel field reporters come to mind. So do ghost hunters."*

And as the cloud-to-cloud lightning transforms the early morning sky over rural Coles County from a bottomless flat black to retina-searing strobes of white, while thunder emanates like bass from some cosmic subwoofer, the paranormal investigators and film crew that have invaded the area's spookiest asylum smile excitedly, savoring the comfort of the familiar.

*"We always seem to have thunderstorms,"* said Philip Adrian Booth, who, with his twin brother, Christopher Saint Booth, makes documentaries about supposedly haunted places.
*"It's a rocking place to shoot a film."*

In fact, the only member of this ensemble not thrilled with the inclement weather is their soft-spoken gadget guy, a retired electrical engineer who scurries to put plastic tarps over cables leading to homemade high-powered lasers as rain begins to leak through the crumbling plaster on the ceiling.

It's July 3 — barely — at Ashmore Estates east of Charleston, and the production crew from California-based Spooked Television Releasing has just wrapped up shooting of promotional footage for the Syfy Channel documentary, "Children

112

of the Grave II." Set for release next year, the film follows "Rock-n-roll Ghost Hunter" Keith Age and his fellow sleuths as they probe eerie confines like old boarding houses and deserted schools.

They're at Ashmore Estates for an overnight shoot because of the one-time mental institution's reputation for paranormal activity. Reportedly built near the site of a fatal schoolhouse fire, Ashmore Estates is now a tourist destination — especially in the fall, when previous owners Scott and Tanya Kelley and about 65 actors stage their annual "haunted house."

But it's also a draw for people looking for real ghosts — people like Juli Velazquez, president of the Illinois Chapter of the International Society of Paranormal Investigators. Based out of Chicago, she has already convened half-a-dozen classes at Ashmore Estates since the beginning of this year. Of the six locales she visits, Velazquez said Ashmore Estates *"is probably my favorite because of all the (paranormal) activity."*

The production crew also enlisted the help of Rick Hayes, who claims abilities as a psychic medium. *When I walked in I felt that this is my last home,"* he said after arriving at Ashmore Estates. *"The words 'last home' - this was a home for many.... this was their last place before they moved on to a different place of their lives."*

According to Ashmore Estate's website, more than 100

people died at the mansion when it served as the Coles County Poor Farm during the first half of the 20th century.

Rounding out the team's key players is Bill Chappell, owner of the small company Digital Dowsing in Loveland, Colorado. Now semi-retired, the former electrical engineer devotes much of his time to building equipment specifically designed for measuring and recording the paranormal.

On this hunt, Chappell, has brought along several lasers that he's arranged in a "convergence" pattern to detect entities in the upstairs hallway of Ashmore Estates. The green laser's beam, in fact, emits at such a low frequency that prolonged exposure holds the potential for tissue damage, Chappell cautions.

*"We're trying to set up a grid so if something walks through it, you will be able to determine its shape (or) its shadow."*

He also fabricated several devices that react to anomalies in the environment's electromagnetic field. This equipment is connected to a computerized 2,000-word dictionary, and generates two-word responses to questions. If these answers are "contextual" — if they make sense under the circumstances — then the ghost hunters are led to believe that something other than their presence is affecting the EM field.

For example, Philip Booth said he asked the device a question and it replied, *"Lady Burn,"* which he interpreted as a reference to the schoolhouse fire fatality that supposedly occurred near the location of Ashmore Estates in the late 19th century.

Surprisingly, Chappell appears to be the most skeptical member of this ghost-chasing cadre. *"I don't make a lot of claims about these devices," he said. "I think people jump to conclusions too quickly."*

But this doesn't mean he is close-minded on the subject of the supernatural. An avid poker player, he said the contextual responses to his EM tools alone defy the odds.

*"I've seen enough to realize something really is going on but I'm not quick to jump out and say it's a departed spirit,"* Chappell said.

He also acknowledges that many of the two-word replies are nonsensical. For example, when asked, *"Are you here?"* the machine answers, *"Slowly frigid." "Descend Betty" is the response to "Is this real?"*

*"It would be a hard stretch to make that (contextual), but you will get people here who will do whatever it takes in their head to make it contextually correct,"* Chappell said.

After setting up their equipment on the night of July 2, the crew records promotional and dramatic reenactment footage: Think fog machines, flashlights and spooky music.

Then they make their way upstairs to the laser grid, where they let the video cameras roll freely. And something happens, they say, although they're not sure what. The Booth brothers and Age will evaluate the video and the data collected by Chappell later.

Age is also armed with a thermal camera, he and Kelley venture into one of the more notorious rooms of Ashmore Estates. Kelley reports seeing shapes that resemble human heads and torsos — which show up on the thermal Imager as colder, darker blues than the cold, dark blue of the room's wall — appearing, moving around and then dissipating.

However, Kelley said the ghost hunters are holding off on certifying Ashmore Estates as truly haunted. *"I can appreciate that,"* he said.

*"We won't come unless it's has some serious credibility,"* said Christopher Booth.

Kelley said the Spooked Television crew is the 15th investigative team to tackle Ashmore Estates during his 2 ½ years as co-owner. *"Every group that has been here has said this place is active, definitely."*

# THE STRANGE CASE OF THE STANLEY HOTEL

The Stanley Hotel in beautiful Estes Park, Colorado known as the inspiration behind Steven King's, "The Shining" was where we premiered "Children Of The Grave 2."

Night of the Super Moon, I checked into Room 217, the room that Steven King stayed when he was working on "The Shining." I very much enjoyed the craw foot bathtub in which I almost drowned in being that its oversized. I kept expecting the sexy to the not so sexy deteriorating woman to step out of the water but unfortunately the closest thing we got was Keith Age investigating the bathroom in which we did not get much activity but Keith was able to get a bath. Room 217 in general felt quite comfortable even though it seemed like the bed kept making itself. With camera equipment in the room we never let the maids enter and clean up the room but every time we returned the bed was made. The front desk assured me there was no maid service.

It is known that in room 217 the bed makes it self. I wish my bed at home would do that.

# THE STRANGE CASE OF THE SOUL CATCHER

It is said that soulcatchers are a spiritual object constructed of a tube of bear femur, incised on one or both sides, and often ornamented with abalone shell. Bears had powerful shamanic connotations among the people of the Northwest Coast. Dreaming, which was thought to be the soul leaving the body and traveling to the spirit world. If the soul was unable to return to the body by morning (due to disorientation or supernatural interference), chronic illness would follow. To cure the patient, the shaman would wear the soulcatcher as a necklace. He would then travel to the spirit world by calling helper spirits using trance music, employing helper-spirit masks, and magical implements such as staffs. Once the errant soul was located, the shaman would "suck" the soul into the soulcatcher, and return to the patient. The soul would then be blown back.

Anita Tallbull with help of the Elders on the Arapaho Indian Reservation allowed us to embark on an adventure of an afterlife time. This has been one of the most soul driven journeys to date in the search for "The Soul Catcher."

Starting out in the dry heated Mojave Desert landing in El Reno, Oklahoma, we went on a search for the history, hauntings and plight of the first Americans. This was my first experience flying in an experimental antique prop plane. This plane was made out of guerrilla tape and refurbished parts. We flew across the endless dry dessert. It's a funny thing, it took so much guts to get me up in the air that in the end I didn't want to come down. Coming down would mean landing, something I didn't believe would happen because one of the landing wheels didn't work. After a good kick from my boot, the wheel released and we finally set down on the dry lake bed.

Exploring the burnt out buildings once known as Indian boarding schools we researched the holocaustic similarities of the conditions they faced brought a valid understanding that this was genocide. The spiritual native way of life is something I have always been connected too. No one is closer to the Earth than these spiritual warriors. I love the culture, the values and their dress. So much spirit has been broken but still you can't keep a good human down.

*"The reduction of the North American Indian population from an estimated 12 million to barely 237,000 represents a vast genocide, the most sustained on record."*

This investigation provided something we had never captured before. We all have had experiences with black shadow people but what about white shadow people? We witnessed a white entity dancing around, parading underneath an abandoned boarding school bleacher. Could it be an angel? Our team consisted of Philip Adrian Booth, Keith Age, Melvin and Anita Tall bull, Adrian and Tina Scalf.

We were honored to interview the elders of the reservation and found their stories truly captivating. Indians are born hunters. No one tells a ghost story better than a Native American. With a heritage so strong and proud is was important that we told the chilling story from their perspective. Granted access by the Arapaho and Apache reservation I had never met more passionate people. The haunting past revealed a great respect for this vanishing race.

*"Look over there, that's where you should point your cameras,"* the Elders said. We grabbed the Thermal Imager and video camera and headed over too where the Native gathering now was. We had been looking for what we were told were shadow warriors. Large shadow figures possibly 20 feet tall. The Native American team were a step ahead of us and already honoring the spirits by offering them a gift of tobacco. How was it possible that they knew exactly where to look? We powered up the FLIR and there stood a large shadow figure right in front of us. We could see the investigator's body heat in the thermal as they were placing their gifts down on the ground for the spirits. Hovering over them was a huge ominous shadow. The images we were capturing resembled a Native American warrior complete with braided hair and moccasin boots. Indian burial grounds were close by so we needed to tread gently as we did not want to upset the spirit guardians.

Meanwhile, filming in the school auditorium a teenage boy

broke the exit door down with just one kick trying to get in. He possessed amazing strength and was said to be controlled by a dark violent spirit. As I tried to interview him that night, the camera would not stay in focus and I will never forget his eyes. *"Do not look into his eyes"* I was told by our Native team. He had eyes of the devil. Burn Devil was graffitied all over the school walls. We had documented *"Burn Devil"* also on the Ovilus communication device.

Anita Tallbull, our Native American Investigator describes the boy.

*"He threw his head back and his arms went out and started jerking a little bit. And he raised his head up his eyes were pure white and he started shaking his head around. I was scared."*

A blessing of sorts was needed. It was time for a smudging. Native American ceremonies use certain herbs usually bound with string into a small bundle. The herbs are burned as part of a ritual or ceremony and are traditionally used to purify or bless people and places. In this case to cleanse and repel evil influence. We were also invited to participate in the sweat lodge that night. A place to get answers and guidance by asking spiritual entities, the Creator and Mother Earth for needed wisdom and power.

Dream Catchers also have been a strong fascination for me. While living in Malibu, California I would collect them and hang them all over my beach front property. Being governed and protected by this spiritual shield maintained me from going completely over the edge. Being a producer as well as an artist has a tendency to split you apart. One is trying to save why the other is trying to spend. An artist disburse ones talent to seek self-satisfaction that we are creating something that we hope will inspire not to mention it keeps us sane.

# THE STRANGE CASE OF PARANOIA

Living in Malibu as an eccentric artist I had seen a lot of strange and questionable things. Whether it was mysterious creatures high in the mountains or soaring UFO's in the beach night sky. I had an interesting friend (to put it lightly) who lived in the guest house who would place large quartz crystals he had gotten from Indonesia all around his dwelling to ward off "evil spirits" as he called them. He had sworn to me many times he was being watched from the trees by strange beings. Extraterrestrial life possibly, hidden only by the fact they had the ability to mimic their surroundings. Curious by my friend's visions, I decided to monitor the situation that night.

I camped outside next to our manmade waterfall and waited. Studying every aspect of these towering palm trees I could see every detail in the moonlight. Starting from the bottom to the top I scaled every inch waiting for some kind of irregularity or movement. That's when I saw what appeared to be eyes. Strange eyes that appeared to be of a reptilian nature. Shocked and disorientated, I could not believe what I was seeing. Still as mouse, I held my breath and waited for the eyes next move. Suddenly it became clear to me that these reptile eyes were a part of something big and something alien was perched in that tree. It had a translucent body that was that of a man size lizard and had the ability to camouflage itself. There appeared to be several of them in the trees. As they cautiously moved I could see they seemed to be studying me as well.

Alien abduction narratives sometimes allege contact with reptilian creatures and we have had our fair sightings of UFOs across the pacific coast ocean. I had seen many a grey unidentified flying object with jet fighters in tow. For the locals it was just another day at the beach.

The next night I decided to grab my binoculars and see if I could witness them again this time tucked away indoors safely behind my backyard window. I had a large window in the back of my house, a 180 degree scenic view of the hills of Zuma State Park. This sparse rugged park provided hiking & equestrian trails, a visitor center & scenic canyon vistas.

My eyes seemed to be focused only on my neighbor's house about 200 feet away set in the hills. They had a small newly built house with a wood deck. On that deck was an old rocking chair illuminated only by a porch light. The hills were lit by the moon and the stars as it was a clear night with visibility at 100%. One has the habit to take for granted the beauty one can see without the light pollution from the city.

With my eyes now focused on the whole hillside, the house, the deck and the chair. I witnessed what appeared to be a dark entity running across the trail only to stop at the wooden deck of the house and engulf the rocking chair in complete blackness. Suddenly the porch light flickered and the entity started to mutate, replicating the chairs form. Once it learned its curves and design, it became the chair's perfect shadow. It is important to note that during this event that evening the chair did not cast a shadow previously even from the porch light until that moment of conception. It is like, the darkness, the entity hid in the shadows waiting, watching and learning. And what it learns, it becomes. How long before it becomes the chair itself?

But don't worry "*IT*" can't hurt us......as it hasn't learned to yet!

# THE STRANGE CASE OF THE HINSDALE HOUSE

One of the coolest parts about what I do is that I get to travel and document the unknown in the craziest places. I was invited to do an investigation by Lara Calhoun at the haunted Hinsdale House. Located in Hinsdale, New York there has been reports of dancing ghosts, drownings, unexplained angelic singing in the woods and a young woman ghost walking around this creepy house. It was said there was also an exorcism performed in the small bedroom with many shadow entities living in the walls.

When I arrived it was like a flooded music festival of sorts. Woodstock came to mind as the wall to wall tents sat in the front and back yard of this decrepit house ready for the all night investigation. The grounds were partially flooded due to the heavy rainfall but that didn't stop a variety of paranormal enthusiasts now covered in mud from camping out to try and catch a ghost.

Young and old alike attended this event, grandmothers, mothers and children. One of the families invited me to stay with them in their tent which I felt was not professionally fitting because there were three generations of women that all had a crush on me.

Accompanied by paranormal investigator Keith Age and the lovely Nini Grace, we had planned a thorough investigation that night. Nini Grace is a Spiritual Teacher, Soul Healer, Trance

126

Medium and Founder of The Enlightenment Center in New Jersey.

The investigation included a tour though the entire abandoned house. The paint was peeling, floorboards were coming up and the bathroom was - well let's just say, it was a work of art. The house reminded me of a crack house or a hideout featured in an Alien Zombie fighting game. It needed a lot of work but had an incredible spooky charisma. Featured on the Discovery Channel this 100 year old house proved to be full of activity.

Nini Grace went on to channel a spirit that literally had me shaking that evening. I was sitting on a chair behind her in the kitchen filming as she was meditating and communicating with what seemed to be one of the spirits of the house. Suddenly my chair started shaking violently. All four legs were off its rocker. Nini began to cry as the energy level grew darker. There was something in front of us we could not see but definitely feel. It was probably the most intense feeling of 'off kilter' I have ever felt besides the Exorcist House. Was there possibly a Vortex (doorway to another realm) here? There was water close by - a small lake where it was said that a small girl had drowned.

My feeling was it was not necessarily the house that was active but it was the land itself, taking over, restoring itself back to its original roots before man had corrupted the grounds. Walking around the property I felt an emptiness, this house was in desperate need of redemption. There was something definitely roaming here, but what? I could smell the lake and the deep dark woods that held its secrets. I couldn't help but think that any clues that we may uncover would be extremely misunderstood. Something terrible happened here whether it was in the house or on the property. The movement in the house we had experienced was a sign of much needed change. We never did find out what exactly happened but one thing is for sure if you have the guts to stay after the sun goes down, don't forget to pack your bag....*your body bag*.

# THE STRANGE CASE OF THE OVILUS

Ovilus... A fascinating device indeed.

The Ovilus built by Digital Dowsing is designed by the talented genius Bill Chappell, a previous robotics engineer. This hand held device is known to capture spirit communications. This cool toy described as "For entertainment purposes only" converts environmental readings into speech based on changes to its sensors. Stocked with a dictionary of words up to 1000 plus, the Ovilus speaks with a human sounding voice reacting to energy. Since my use of this device, the Ovilus has had many upgrades over the course of years and your Ovilus may have many more words. As for the *"For Entertainment Purposes Only"* label it is used as a helpful tool along with the rest of your evidence and cannot be relied on fully by itself.

Though one cannot say that the words used as evidence gathered from this device is 100% credible, it shouldn't be written off neither. With the revolution from the original Ovilus to the Ovilus 5 as well as the iOvilus Apps. I have found through our extensive use of this device that it's either spot on and will blow you away or completely irrelevant, spitting out a lot of words that seem random but basically has nothing to do with your investigation's subject matter, or does it?

Speaking from experience, we used the Ovilus 1 and

Paranormal Puck in many of our Syfy productions, "The Possessed," "Soul Catcher," "The Exorcist File" and "Children Of The Grave 2."

The readings we got back in my opinion were very useful and provided possible answers or clues on where to head next in our investigation, but should also be taken with a grain of salt. For us it seemed factual at least 50% of the time. I remember testing it by taking the Ovilus into a hotel room and pointing it around till it spoke. The words that came out of this slick box was *"Phil, hot, lamp"*. Sure enough there was Philip my brother sitting by the lamp who had just burned himself by accidentally touching the light bulb from the hotels bedside lamp. When used in other paranormal investigations it would say words like *"molest, incest, rape, etc."* when we were reviewing a possible sexual abuse case. Though one could not use this as 100% credible proof, the investigator could research further to see if that did indeed occur. Then they could ask more sensitive questions with that subject matter in mind, like in an EVP session in hopes to find closure for the violated.

What I do want to point out is, is it possible that this hand held ECM (Environmental Communications Mode) unit is able to pick up the users thoughts or energy? For instance say you are looking for a ghost girl named Mary. Despite the fact that every ghost girl seems to be named Mary, you would ask, *"Is your name Mary?"* or you might ask, *"What is your name?"* The Ovilus would then sound off. If your spirit is in tune you may get a word like *"yes"* or even the name *"Mary"* or another name. Can one justify

130

that as credible evidence in form of communication from the other side if you get what you were looking for?

As this is just my personal view, I believe that the Ovilus in some way can read your personal environmental energy as well. Meaning it may pick up your thoughts or even read your mind. For instance; if you are looking for a ghost named Mary, it may say "*Mary*" because you are thinking of the name Mary or visualizing this in your thoughts. Now keeping this in mind, how can we ever be sure if it's indeed the ghost of Mary actually communicating or the Ovilus is simply picking up our thoughts?

No one knows for sure how these devices work or if even they work at all. At the end of the day it could be all just some spooky coincidence. With an Ouija board, Franks Box etc. you basically have a question in need of an answer. Trapped spirits communicate through energy whether it's a flashlight, battery drain, dowsing rods, pendulums, white noise or an Ovilus. With that theory now arising, it is not out of the question to think that any form of commutative device could be manipulated by a spirit or our energy. Also, when it comes to the Ovilus words that are not programmed into the software, not only are spoken but will show up on the DTD aka Digital Text Display (for example, walking through a house the Ovilus would spit out "*fuck*," " *shit*," and "*fag*"). How do we explain that? I believe the older forms of unmodified Ovilus are more correct than the phone Apps. Though we may never know for sure if it's the spirits trying to contact us or it's our mind contaminating the intangible airwaves.

Either way there is a valid reason to use these forms of communications as long as we are getting some kind of answers, movement and clues to continue our search for the afterlife.

*'In the magical universe there are no coincidences and there are no accidents. Nothing happens unless someone wills it to happen.'* ~ William S Burroughs

# THE STRANGE CASE OF THE END, OR THE NEW BEGINNING?

Throughout my decade of being involved with the paranormal field I have had the pleasure to meet many dedicated paranormal investigators. Denise Mendenhall is a paranormal enthusiast. We agree to agree in many aspects on the right way to approach the unexplained.

Denise shares her theory;

*"When investigating the paranormal and teaching at the colleges, I have always said, one must rule out the normal before looking to the paranormal. As investigators, it is critical that we look at natural disturbances and occurrences within the locations before pulling out the gear and diving straight into investigative mode."*

*"At times, teams will jump to the conclusions that everything is paranormal say almost anything to obtain an investigation - to the point of frightening people into allowing an investigation to occur."*

*"How do I know this? I have taken too many late night phone calls, answer emails and spoken with people who are scared silly after speaking or working with some teams."*

*"As investigators, we should be "the calm in the middle of the storm" not creating the storm! Professional behavior requires*

that we reassure them that we will do our best to provide them with answers, not scare them more. There are many times that investigations are NOT warranted. There are even times when it is in the best interests of the family that a team does no investigation. However, due to lack of proper interviewing skills, it may not be discovered until it is too late. Mental health issues of a family member being one of the top reasons a team does not belong doing an investigation. One may be opening themselves and their team into some serious legal issues."

"At locations where there is paranormal activity, I am troubled with how many teams treat the spirits. Spirits were people too. They were someone's mother, father, brother, sister, daughter and son. One day, we may be one as well. How do you want to be treated if you are earthbound?"

"I certainly do not want my family or myself taunted, teased or provoked. Sadly, it is happening still. We are teaching our children not to bully on the playground, and yet these rules are not applying to the spirits. How sad."

"Teams should be attempting to discover the messages that the spirits may have, deliver them if possible and ask the spirits to go to the light. Many of these spirits are earthbound for one reason or another. Why not help them find peace so they can move on? Would you want to be earthbound and tortured for years or possibly eternity?"

"Lastly, there is aftercare. So many teams will obtain an investigation and gather the evidence and the client or family will *not hear from them again if they cannot continually investigate the location. We all have the responsibility to do adequate follow up with those that place their confidence in us as investigators. Making a few phone calls and emails inquiring about how things are going show you truly care. If you don't care about the people - perhaps paranormal investigating isn't something you should be doing. This field is about the spirits, the story and the people who came to us with their concerns or fears and they deserve to have some form of proper care and respect."*

Imagine investigating a location where a brutal murder took place. The ghost or spirits said to haunt are the victims of this horrific slaying. Shouldn't our main priority be to help these poor souls move on and get closure? Not exploit them by putting them on public display like some kind of freak show. If my house was haunted by a murdered soul my only goal would be to help them move toward the light.

I never understood the drama that goes on in the paranormal community. It is supposed to be about the spirits, the ghosts and the lost souls. It's not about the ghost hunters or the location owners. The word 'hunter' in general is derogatory as ghosts are not trophies. There are no experts in the paranormal field only seasoned professionals. If I needed a doctor to help me get better, I would look for one that has had a lot of experience, one that had compassion and one I could trust. The same goes in any field as far as I am concerned. The older, the wiser may come into play here as my respect for a seasoned demonologist ranks far above an ordained newbie. I mean no disrespect to any ordained newbies that may read this.

As science can be explained it really is not a part of paranormal at all except to disprove...so when you utilize these scientific gadgets there has to be a form of belief even with the technology.

**Science in the paranormal field should be used to assist not to rule.** The paranormal world is spirit based. If you are not spiritual then I very much doubt you will truly be successful in contacting the other side. That gut feeling, your intuition are the things you were born with and need to trust. Sad, happy, love and injustice are the four points of my paranormal compass through these dark halls of loss. It is what I feel in my heart that determines my soul's direction. One must have compassion for the living to respect the dead. We are not there to grave dance, we are there to find the missing pieces that completes the puzzle of closure for the afterlife. We need to work all together as one. Only then we will find that the paranormal expert is no one.

I had studied many Ascended Master Teachings to help me find my way through the dark times in my life including Buddhism, Saint Germain and The Violet Flame/Violet Fire. I have read the books of Dalai Lama and Eckhart Tolle front to back. Whether it was 108 chants of *"Om Mani Padme Hum"* or the affirmation *"I AM a being of violet fire, I AM the purity God's desire,"* I was covered. I'm sure you already know the names of a few ascended masters such as Jesus Christ, Gautama Buddha and Krishna. I found these teachings to be great resources for self-transformation. After all who is the ultimate Holy Ghost but Jesus himself?

I recommend meditation before you and your team enter a spirit zone. Leave your baggage at the door for where you going they are just containers full of emotion.

You see I believe that everyone is sensitive per-say. How much you are willing to develop and practice your gift leads to your fullest potential. Artists such as painters, writers, musicians etc., communicate through their emotions which in turn creates a dramatic masterpiece. Their world is their canvas and their ups and downs are their paint. Artists need to be in touch with their sensitive side in order to survive. Yes, you guessed it. Women, children and artists are more open to the paranormal due to the fact that they are true to their emotions. They are spiritual souls controlled by their heart not by their mind.

Later I would learn this introverted outlook I perceived was that of a HSP, a highly sensitive person.


*"A highly sensitive person (HSP) is a person having the trait of high sensory processing sensitivity. This is a specific trait, with key consequences for how we view people, that in the past has often been confused with innate shyness, social anxiety problems."*

Elaine Aron ~ The Highly Sensitive Person

When you are born, your soul is flawless like a mirror with clear perception. Like an innocent child, it reflects everything around you as happy and new. As you grow up you begin to nourish on life's experiences. Whether it's the people, food or drink, these needs and surroundings can fog the soul's reflection. To the point that your inner light becomes cloudy and your soul no longer casts a clear picture. Love becomes hate, giving turns to greed and we listen with a new formed ego. Judgement becomes just that, judging.

It's important not to feed on other people's perceptions of you. Believe in yourself and follow that gut feeling. There's a reason why the higher power gave you intuition. Intuition is the kill switch to make sure your light does not burn out. As the saying goes, "*God knows I'm good*" but in this case, you know you're good because you speak with authority and that authority is your heart.

We must all remember when it comes to paranormal investigations, it's about respect and most of all closure. It is not about fame, drama, or the ghost hunting t-shirt. Who cares if you're on TV when you're saving someone's soul? Be the true hero. When you really want to help and communicate with the spirit of a lost one, we must focus on just that - the lost souls. Otherwise, join team Jersey Shore or investigate with TMZ. I would never invite them into my life never mind my house. Paranormal friends, please keep it real, be respectful and compassionate and remember you are dealing with someone's hereafter.

Like all of our paranormal cases, we don't really care that it is haunted, **we care why it is haunted**. We set out and became the first to bring cameras inside to show you the viewer, the truth, the real events and elements. To help fill in the gaps of what seemed to be an unbelievable story. History is far more haunting when told right. You go after a story only to come across another story that is far more interesting and scary. Think of it like this, a story is like a tree that has many branches and roots, once uncovered you unearth its deep buried secrets. They lead us to the root (heart) of the matter, from the tree of the afterlife. S.O.S does not stand for Save Our Selves.

For us mere mortals the adventures have just begun, but for the lost souls, without closure it never ends.

~~The End~~

THE BEGINNING!

# ABOUT THE AUTHOR

Christopher Saint Booth born in Yorkshire, England started his career at an early age. Influenced by The Beatles, singing and strumming at the age of four. Atlantic crossing brought them to Canada where at the age of thirteen he were writing and performing at the local establishments. In 1978 he was invited to combine forces with, Juno award winner, Sweeney Todd. (London Records) Worldwide touring commenced immediately as their new gold album paved his way to sunny California. Upon arriving in Los Angeles, greeted with a publishing deal (RCA Music) he began writing vocalizations and musical scores for film, cable and television.

Desires of new creative outlets began development, now reaching out to the visual side of entertainment. Audio with Video studios were soon built to quench this creative thirst.

Internationally renowned for his provocative style, Independent films soon broadened the horizon. Financing a million-dollar HD digital domain in Los Angeles California, this is where he would design and build his ultimate dreams. As well as endorsed by an array of electronic arts manufacturers, no boundaries would be left untouched. For every new technical toy that the eyes and ears could ever dream of soon became vivid. As an Apple licensed developer and 3rd party designer for SoftImage, AMP, APDA and Microsoft, Booth continued to design the future of entertainment and media for all platforms. New concepts with slick designs go hand in hand with the latest web and mobile technology.

With over 100 features behind him built all from scratch with the insight of what's happening tomorrow for the people today. A panoramic view of freedom with the fresh scent of change inspires this Saint to create a brave new world for your eyes and ears.

Credits include Producer and Director of films and documentaries for Syfy, Chiller, NBC Universal, Spooked TV Productions, At&t, Vimeo, Apple iTunes, Netflix, Roku and more worldwide. CEO of Spooked Television and Twintalk Entertainment.

Films include Dead Still (Syfy), Death Tunnel (Sony Pictures), The Possessed, Spooked, Children Of The Grave (Syfy Channel/ NBC Universal), The Exorcist File-Haunted Boy (Redbox), Children Of The Grave 2, Soul Catcher and DarkPlace

Christopher is married to Rachel and the father to Gabriel and Alyss.

## THANKS TO

Keith Age and the LGHS
Rosemary Ellen Guiley ~ Anita Tallbull ~ Nini Grace
John Zaffis ~ Rick Hayes ~ Gregory Myers ~ Sandy Oates ~
Robbin Terry ~ Sharon Coyle ~ John Whitman ~ Joyce Wesbrooks
Charlie and Tina Mattingly ~ Mary Ellen Hammack ~ Barry Taff
Juli Velazquez ~Laura Calhoun ~ Rob Johnson ~ Steven LaChance
Dewi Morgaine ~ Bill Chappell ~ Dave Schrader ~ Russell Stum
Chris Fleming ~ Ray Cannella ~ Scott Kelley ~ Marcus Chatman
Troy Taylor ~ Betsy Belanger ~ Ron Parkhurst ~ Callea Sherrill
William Bradshaw Ph.D ~ Kathy Reno ~ Richard Novosak ~Eileen
Dryer ~ Charles and Deloris Webster ~ Viki Main~ Michael Lynch
~ Thomas Sachy ~ Michael Kleen~
Arapaho Indian Reservation

## SPECIAL THANKS

Denise Mendenhall
Philip Adrian Booth
Johnny B
Bishop James Long
and
Rachel Marie Booth

## IN MEMORY OF

Anika ~ Brian K. Wilson Sr.
Matthew McGrory ~ Donn Shy
Ronald Thornburry ~ Tom Halstead
Frank Sumption ~ Rev. Francis X. Cleary
Grand-Mum Jackson ~ Leslie Booth
Mark Tallbear and
Audrey Jackson Booth

# REFERENCES

Rob Stroud and Nathaniel West of Journal Gazette Times/Courier
Bancroft Hunt, Norman. "Shamanism in North America." 2002.
Firefly Books. Buffalo.
Wardwell, Allen. "Tangible Visions: Northwest Coast Shamanism
and its Art." 1996
The Monticelli Press. New York.


http://www.cdc.gov/tb/

http://theenlightenmentcntr.com/nini/

http://en.wikipedia.org/wiki/Ashmore_Estates

http://en.wikipedia.org/wiki/Wikipedia:Text_of_Creative_Commo
ns_Attribution-ShareAlike_3.0_Unported_License

http://jg-tc.com/news/article_a363299b-2831-53a7-8dd2-1a6c9397
498d.html

http://jg-tc.com/news/article_c0e6c9a9-f45c-50d9-8b4a-cc4a63074
e61.html

http://hsperson.com/

# PARANORMAL LOCATIONS

Linda Vista Hospital - Los Angeles, CA

Waverly Hills Sanatorium - Louisville, KY

Crown Hill Cemetery - Indianapolis, IN

Bartonville State Asylum - Peoria, IN

Manteno State Asylum- Manteno, IL

Glore Psychiatric Museum- St. Joseph, MO

Ashmore Estates - Ashmore, IL

Rolling Hills Asylum- Bethany, NY

Watseka Wonder House- Watseka, IL

Exorcist House- Bel-nor, MO

Hinsdale House- Hinsdale, NY

Queen Mary- Long Beach, CA

The Crescent Hotel- Eureka Springs, AR

The Stanley Hotel- Estes Park, CO

The Old Soldiers Home -Westwood, CA

Zombie Road- St. Louis, MO

The Mayfair Hotel- St. Louis, MO

Lemp Mansion- St. Louis, MO

# SPOOKED TV PRESENTS

Feature Films, Documentaries and Music
DVD's

**www.spookedtv.com**

SPOOKEDtv-OD Powered by VIMEO
**www.vimeo.com/spookedtvod/vod_pages**

ORIGINAL SOUNDTRACKS
iTunes
**www.itunes.apple.com/us/artist/christopher-saint/id211036282**

CD Baby
**www.cdbaby.com/Artist/ChristopherSaint1**

## DARKPLACE

Winner of Best Feature Film Chicago Film Festival

Official Selection Gasparilla Film Festival

A hillbilly giant and the local preacher exorcise their ritual of dark cleansing by using an ancient box forcing you to face your inner demons. But when a 10 year old boy is locked up inside, his darkest fears sets loose an inferno of relentless evil. Starring, Matthew McGrory (Devil's Rejects,Big Fish) in his last screen performance, Katherine Boecher (Supernatural), Dougald Park, Irwin Keyes and Timothy Lee DePriest

**www.vimeo.com/ondemand/darkplace**

## SPOOKED

### The Ghosts Of Waverly Hills Sanatorium

As seen on the Syfy. This highly acclaimed documentary follows Hollywood filmmakers as they uncover the shocking history within the haunted halls of "The Scariest Place On Earth", Waverly Hills Sanatorium, a monster of a building where it is said over 63,000 people died. Some say the DEAD are still there!

**www.vimeo.com/ondemand/spooked**

**DEATH TUNNEL** (Sony Pictures)

Winner of Best Horror Film. Fantastic Film Festival

Official Selection LA Screamfest Film Festival

For an initiation stunt, five college women are locked in a
Kentucky hospital built in 1910 where 63,000 people died from a
disease known as the "white plague". Deep under the hospital is
the "Death Tunnel" which once were used to remove the dead.

**www.deathtunnel.com**

**CHILDREN OF THE GRAVE**

As seen on Syfy. Winner of Best Paranormal Documentary.

Uncovers the shocking truth, history and haunting of
Ghost Children, Poltergeist Kids, Haunted Orphanages and
Crybaby Bridges through untold stories of unmarked graves.

**www.childrenofthegrave.com**

## THE POSSESSED

As seen on Syfy. Winner of Best Paranormal Documentary.

Based on the True Story, The Watseka Wonder, America's first documented possession in 1870. A chilling story of a 13-year-old girl from the small town of Watseka, Illinois who became possessed by spirits of the insane dead.

**www.thepossessedmovie.com**

**www.vimeo.com/ondemand/thepossessed**

## THE EXORCIST FILE - HAUNTED BOY

As seen in RedBox.(Top Rental 2014)
Winner of Best Feature Film-Full Moon Horror Film Festival.

While filming a haunted asylum in St. Louis, Missouri, documentary filmmakers uncover a secret diary of the infamous 1949 exorcism involving a 13 year old boy possessed by the devil that later inspired the book and movie "The Exorcist".

**www.theexorcistfile.com**

**www.vimeo.com/ondemand/theexorcistfile**

**Now on iTunes**

**CHILDREN OF THE GRAVE II**

Official Selection Gasparilla Film Festival

The true hauntings of ghost children and their emotional stories of the supernatural continues.

**www.childrenofthegrave2.com**

**www.vimeo.com/ondemand/cotg2**


**SOUL CATCHER**

Travel across gothic landscapes and uncover the haunting stories of abandoned Indian boarding schools built to imprison the once free spirit of Native Americans. Uncover ghosts, shape shifters and shadow people.

**www.soulcatchermovie.com**

**www.vimeo.com/ondemand/soulcatcher**

## THE UNSEEN
## BEST OF THE BOOTH BROTHERS

The Unseen showcases the best of all their films and docs.
Watch what the networks wouldn't dare to air. Share the tears,
the fears, the laughs and jumps in this shocking uncut
collection of their infamous films hosted by the Booth Brothers

**www.vimeo.com/ondemand/unseen**

**DEAD STILL** (Syfy)

Official Selection Gasparilla Film Festival

Official Selection Orlando Florida Walker Stalker Film Festival

Upon the death of his great grandfather, Brandon
Davis a wedding photographer inherits an antique camera famous
for taking Victorian death photography. After photographing his
subjects they start to die from horrible, bizarre deaths.
Starring Ben Browder (Farscape, Stargate), Ray Wise (Twin
Peaks, Jeepers Creepers), Elle LaMont (Machette Kills, Dusk Till
Dawn) and Gavin Casalegno (Noah, When The Game Stands Tall).

**www.dead-still.com**

## GINGER NUTS OF HORROR UK INTERVIEW WITH CHRISTOPHER SAINT BOOTH By Joe Young

GNOH: Your most recent release in the U.K. is "Dead Still" (Distributor: ContentMediaUK.), the story of a photographer with a most unusual camera. I have to say from the start that it is one of the best films I have seen this year. It stars Ben Browder (Farscape) and Ray Wise (Twin Peaks, Reaper) in an effectively creepy chiller with story line and visual elements reminiscent of the Twilight Zone and Silent Hill. Looking at the behind the scenes material it appears as if you the Booth Brothers are two parts of a single machine, each of you providing different skills in the overall process. Did you make a conscious decision for one of you to focus on a differing aspect to the other so that between both of you all of the bases were covered?

CSB: That's what we do on all of our productions. Being identical twins we not only look alike but kinda think alike. That makes it a stronger team. It's like having two cameras covering what's going on, it's easier to cover what's going on and change quickly what's not working on the fly. If you ever said, "I wish I had another like me" well there you go... BOOM!

GNOH: In 'Dead Still' Ray Wise, a veteran of over 90 films, is flawless as the Victorian 'Death Photographer' Wenton Davis, what was he like to work with?

CSB: It was an honor, Ray Wise was perfect for the role. Ray loved the part. He wanted to put his own flair and touch to the character. Ray even grew a beard, studied the past of Victorian Death photography. He has been an inspiration for us with his work in Twin Peaks so when came on board we were like excited school girls, completely in awe. Originally the role was going to be played by Sid Haig but personally Ray Wise nails it. I think it's one of his best roles he's played to date. A super talented actor with passion, charm and charisma, Ray definitely was our villain, our Jack Nicholson per-se in The Shining. Ray brings a lot to the table, an actor of intrigue with a creep factor you need in todays over saturated horror films.

151

GNOH: You both have so many strings to your bows, if you could only concentrate on one aspect of your talents what would it be?

CSB: I think music; a film's score has always played an important role in movie making. Music has always been my first love and second being Production Design in which I do on all of our productions. Also being the Producer on this flick I must deliver the best of the best while keeping on budget and schedule. Creation and passion in anything you do is the key.

GNOH: With all of the horror remakes in the pipeline at the moment from various studios what would be the one remake you wouldn't mind being offered and why?

CSB: Philip and I were courted to do the Texas Chainsaw Massacre remake, the one with Jessica Biel. For some political reason it didn't work out. A lot of that movie has scenes and lighting exactly like our film 'DarkPlace' starring the late Matthew McGrory. I think the 1980 film 'The Entity' starring Barbara Hershey would be a great one to tackle. We actually have been playing around with that one ever since we met Barry Taff the real para-psychologist who studied that creepy case. So you never know, it's on our twisted-bucket list.

GNOH: I know you have said that America has a huge supply of haunted places, but would you ever consider film-making outside of the USA if the right project came along?

CSB: Of course. It just has to be the right story. We like to take on projects that have never been told. It's all about the story and the redemption. Would love to film in Tibet

GNOH: Memento Mori are popular in your films, do you have a favorite piece of your own and if so, what makes it special?

CSB: Yes I collect something from every set and story we have been involved in. For instance, an 18th century prosthetic arm from our paranormal doc 'Children Of The Grave, old clothes and letters from abandoned hospitals we found and of course the diary of the real Exorcist case. Talk about a reality check. When you read the real writings from the real people you are showcasing it's your mission, your duty as a filmmaker, a story teller to get it right.

GNOH : You've had a very interesting time of things, rocking out in front of 20,000 fans, ghost hunting, documentary making, working on albums and videos, making horror movies. Is there something that you dream of doing which is totally unrelated to showbiz?

CSB: Being a spiritual teacher of sorts. Of course not with the fast cars etc, lol, but just inspiring the world not to give up, to stand by one's dreams and never giving up. I think meditation and believing in yourself is so important. I think I just realized this is my Plan B but really should be my Plan A. :) A remix by Skrillex of my life would be perfect.

GNOH: Regarding the paranormal, exploring Waverly Hills Sanatorium was a turning point for you and the genesis of your film 'Death Tunnel', but what were your expectations before going there?

CSB: It's weird as I did not have any expectations. We were just going there to scout a location. But boom when we got there, life changed. 'Introduction to the paranormal 101'. It was eye-opening to witness the paranormal activity there and then try to deal with it when we went back to Los Angeles. I will never forget driving up to Waverly Hills for the first time; It was like finding Frankenstein's castle in the middle of nowhere. What an after-LIFE lesson it was.

GNOH: Was there ever a project you passed up on and regretted your decision?

CSB: Yes, being an Indie film company, one cannot move fast enough sometimes. There have been many projects and stories we were adapting, setting up to shoot and Mr. Big from Hollywood would move in days before. But that's the nature of the beast. It's important not to have yesterday regrets, become cynical and bitter. That will destroy today and days to come. We owned several adaptions of stories that have not been told. For instance; 'The Possessed' the true story of America's first possession, 'The Exorcist File' being first to film inside the real Exorcist house, lead a paranormal investigation and document untold events, 'Death Tunnel' and 'Spooked' to unveil the history and hauntings of Waverly Hills Sanatorium and 'Children Of The Grave' uncovering ghost children in haunted Orphanages. The night and career is young so stay tuned for more mind blowing projects.

GNOH: Your respect for a faithful background to your horror films and documentaries is laudable, has there been a particular person discovered in your research that you felt the most sorrow for?

CSB: I think all of our characters have their own sad stories. Being empathy driven we have a tendency to focus on their spirit to overcome, children being the most difficult. When you have a child of your own and it cries you will do everything to comfort the tearful one but when you are dealing with ghost children how do you comfort them? It's absolutely heartbreaking. All you can do is tell their story and hope it creates closure.

GNOH: In your documentaries and movies you give texture without sensationalizing or using too much gore and too many jump scares. Do you believe that holds you back from becoming more famous?

CSB: We don't make slasher films, nothing against them it just seems like watching the news to me. We prefer good ghost stories with that dark Asian horror feel. I think you can disturb much more by what you don't see. The kill scenes in our films are very gory and disturbing. We prefer to use fear and twisted visions of horror. With that said Dead Still has some great new approaches to sick and twisted deaths.

GNOH: What's the one thing you would never do in one of your films?

CSB: Settle...Don't ever Settle… for bad lighting, bad acting and cheap SFX make up. If budget and time is a concern which it always is, make the call to cut it out, shadow it or rewrite the scene.

GNOH: Exclusive, you heard it here first folks: Can you tell our readers something about yourself  that you have not said in any documentary or in any other interview?

CSB: I've just got married which I never thought I would again as I have been married three times before. It has been an incredible adventure so far to live day by day with your own personal cheerleader. Meaning someone that believes in you and supports the long hours and the dreams of a crazy artist. I recommend if you find that special person never let them go. Salvador Dali had his Gala and now I have mine, my true artistic muse.

GNOH: What general advice would you give to anyone wishing to get into the independent film business?

CSB: Never give up. Don't get so lost in the business of filmmaking that the art suffers. It's important to know the business especially in today's film market but don't cheat yourself from the thrill. Love what you do.

GNOH: Thank you for taking the time out of your busy schedule for this interview, I've had a great time talking with you and I look forward to future offerings.

CSB: Never too busy for you. Loved it cheers.


*This interview was edited. You can find the full interview on the GNOH UK network. Special thanks to GNOH and Joe Young for their continued support.*

SPOOKED TV  PUBLICATIONS
18017 CHATSWORTH STREET #130
GRANADA HILLS, CA 91344
Email: info@spookedproductions.com
Phone: 310-498-9576


VISIT US ON FACEBOOK

**www.facebook.com/SPOOKEDtv**

**www.facebook.com/christophersaintbooth**


TWITTER

**www.twitter.com/spookedtv**


OFFICIAL SITE

**WWW.SPOOKEDTV.COM**


PARANOIA: The Strange Case of Ghosts, Demons and Aliens.
©2015 Spooked Productions

ISBN-10: 0692488901
ISBN-13: 978-0692488904

www.ingramcontent.com/pod-product-compliance
Lightning Source LLC
Chambersburg PA
CBHW072150090426
42740CB00012B/2215